Is There Life After Death?

Is Life Eternal, Endless,
Everlasting, Perpetual?

Start at the Beginning,
Then Decide.

The Bible
Around and Beyond

By Alfred Wagner

AB ASPECT Books

www.ASPECTBooks.com

World rights reserved. This book or any portion thereof may not be copied or reproduced in any form or manner whatever, except as provided by law, without the written permission of the publisher, except by a reviewer who may quote brief passages in a review.

The author assumes full responsibility for the accuracy of all facts and quotations as cited in this book. The opinions expressed in this book are the author's personal views and interpretations, and do not necessarily reflect those of the publisher.

This book is provided with the understanding that the publisher is not engaged in giving spiritual, legal, medical, or other professional advice. If authoritative advice is needed, the reader should seek the counsel of a competent professional.

Copyright © 2015 ASPECT Books
ISBN-13: 978-1-4796-0585-9 (Paperback)
ISBN-13: 978-1-4796-0586-6 (ePub)
ISBN-13: 978-1-4796-0587-3 (Mobi)
Library of Congress Control Number: 2015915009

Published by
AB ASPECT Books
www.ASPECTBooks.com

Introduction

This book encompasses ancient and early religious history in an effort to document in one location the sequence of events from Adam and Eve to the present age. Humanity's existence is a fascinating study, but we must involve our minds if we are to understand the things that surround us. This book examines the writings of the Old and New Testaments, including the consequences and outcome of the events that have shaped world history.

This book has been arranged in the order of time to show the true relation of one event to another. The reason and motive for this work is to present the facts of history.

This book also illustrates the unfolding and the sequence of events, including the consequences and outcome of each, beginning with the prophets and their prophecies as written in the Old Testament. God blessed the Israelites, for they worshiped the one, true God, Creator of heaven and earth. He blessed them through the birth of His Son, Jesus. God also favored the Romans in the building of their empire for a purpose in history.

This book contains excerpts from the Bible and other reference materials such as encyclopedias, dictionaries, and concordances to present an outline of the events that have shaped the history of humanity. It is important that we study ancient and religious history to understand the times we live in.

The information presented in this book was derived from:
- *The American College Encyclopedic Dictionary*. Chicago, IL: The Spencer Press, Inc., 1955.
- Scott, Walter Dill, Franklin J. Meine, and W. Stewart Wallace. *The American Peoples Encyclopedia*. Chicago, IL: The Spencer Press, Inc.,

1956.
- King James Version Bible
- *The New International Standard Medical and Health Encyclopedia.* Edited by Richard J. Wagman. New York, NY: Trident Reference Publishing, 2005.
- *Webster's New World Dictionary.* Edited by David B. Guralnik. Simon and Schuster, 1980.

Contents

Chapter 1	Ancient History Before and After Christ.	9
Chapter 2	Idol Worship and Ancient Gods.	17
Chapter 3	The Building of the Roman Empire.	23
Chapter 4	Christianity and the Roman Catholic Church.	42
Chapter 5	Roman Rule to Muslim Domination	65
Chapter 6	Other World Religions	69
Chapter 7	Communication.	73
Chapter 8	The Three Essentials Sustaining Humanity: Food, Clothing, Shelter.	76
Chapter 9	Minerals and Tools	88
Chapter 10	The Human Race and Human Body	92
Chapter 11	Population of the Earth.	104
Chapter 12	The Holy Spirit	110
Chapter 13	Summaries of This Book's Instances	114
Conclusion	. . . .	133

Chapter 1

Ancient History Before and After Christ

Since humans learned to write, they have inscribed words on a variety of surfaces as a form of communication. From rocks to animal hides to paper, humans throughout history have permanently documented events through the written word.

Writing in the Beginning

The Old Testament gives us a view of life and events from the beginning of the world. Most of the Old Testament was written in the ancient Aramaic Semitic language that was common in that day and age. It is noted that Jesus spoke Aramaic, as did His parents.

Semitic is a subfamily of the Afro-Asiatic family of languages—Hebrew, Arabic, Egyptian—with its influences being felt in a region extending from the Horn of Africa to North Africa to the Middle East. The Semitic alphabet was the basis for the language of the Old Testament of the Bible. Alphabetic writing came to Greece from the Phoenicians, the region of Syria and Egypt, with the earliest known specimens dating to approximately 2000 BC.

Judaism

The Old Testament, or Tanakh, was written in ancient Israel over a period of 1,000 years by many authors. The Jewish religion, a monotheistic religion based on the laws and teachings of the Holy Scriptures and the Talmud, a collection of writings of Jewish, civil, and religious law, is documented within the pages of the Bible.

The Old Testament documents the first humans—Adam and Eve—who lived on this earth and goes through the time of Noah and the flood. It then documents the life of Abraham, the father of the Jewish nation who lived 175 years, and his descendants who carried the promise of one day becoming a great nation.

Palestine

The original inhabitants of Palestine, especially Western Palestine little is known. This land located between the Jordan River, the Dead Sea, and the Mediterranean Sea.

God called: this region the Promised Land, which he devoted to Abram, GEN. 12:1-3; Abram, the son of Shem, who was one of Noah's son's.

Abram, was seventy and five years old when he departed out of Haran as the Lord hath spoken unto him. Along with his wife Sarai, and Lot his brother's son, and all their substance that they had gathered and the persons they hath gotten in Haran; and they went forth to go into the Land of Canaan, and into the Promised Land they came

Canaan

Canaan the son of Ham, and grandson of Noah, GEN. 10:6, and also the land which his descendants, known as Canaanites presently inhabited. The Land: of Canaan originally comprised the low coastland of Palestine on the Mediterranean. At a later period the name Canaan became enlarged to include the whole of Palestine, and was known by the name of these people; the Canaanites.

Canaanite; a member of the Semitic people inhabiting Palestine at the time of the Hebrew encroachment (Semitic is a person regarded as a descended from Shem, one of Noah's sons).

Hundreds of years later the subjugation of the Canaanites, and their land was effected, only by degrees, of the Hebrew encroachment.

Moses

Moses led his people out of bondage in Egypt, across the Red Sea into the wilderness, where they wondered forty years. Jehovah (God), spoke to the people, giving them his commands and providing for their needs.

Because of an incident in which Moses displayed a lack of confidence in God, he was forbidden entrance into the Promised Land of Canaan, (A place where they would have a better life).

Moses died at the age of 120, on top of Mount Nebo, in view of the Promised Land. At that time Joshua became his successor and led the Israelites into the land of Canaan.

Syria and Palestine were annexed to the Roman Empire by Pompey in 63 BC.

After the conquest of Canaan, the Israelites settled into life in their new home. Before long the Jewish nation desired a king to rule like the nations surrounding them. Saul, the first king of Israel, came to the throne sometime near 1030 BC. During his reign he quarreled with David, his son-in-law, the son of Jesse, and sought his life, at which point David fled for his life. However, Saul never caught David, and Saul was eventually defeated by the Philistine at Bilboa, and he took his own life for fear that the Philistines would capture him and torture him.

David succeeded Saul and established a permanent capital in Jerusalem. After David's death, his son Solomon assumed the throne. Unfortunately, after Solomon's reign the nation as a whole collapsed and the next 200 years of history were fraught with revolutions, assassinations, and captivity (732–586 BC).

Isaiah was one of the three, and perhaps greatest, of the major prophets. Living during the eighth century, his prophetic career covered forty years from 740–701 BC. Most of his work was done in Jerusalem. He foretold of the coming Messiah. He complained about the sins of the nation and exhorted the people to repent of their ways. He predicted that Jerusalem would be destroyed and the people carried into captivity.

When Isaiah spoke of Israel as a chosen people, he did not mean that they were, therefore, a favorite people. Israel was chosen only in the sense that they were obligated to live above the average and be examples to all clans, tribes, and nations.

After living a holy life, Isaiah died through martyrdom by being sawed in half in a hollow log at the command of King Manasseh after reproving the king for his evil ways.

Jesus and the apostles refer to Isaiah more than fifty times in the New Testament.

Jeremiah was a Hebrew prophet (*c.* 650–*c.* 585 BC) who lived in imminent danger of death because of his fearless preaching. According to tradition, he was stoned to death in the city of Tahpanhes, Egypt. Stoning was a form of Hebrew capital punishment, not Egyptian.

During Jeremiah's lifetime Nebuchadnezzar reigned over the Babylonian Empire (605–561 BC). Nebuchadnezzar became king of Babylon after his father's death in 604 BC. Babylon is located in what is now south Iraq near the Euphrates River, bounded on the northeast by Turkey. Nebuchadnezzar defeated the Egyptian Army in 605 BC. Seven years after assuming the throne, he destroyed Jerusalem and took 4,000 Jews into captivity. He then invaded and plundered Egypt, restoring Babylon to its former glory with the riches he brought back from his conquests.

In 597 BC when his army captured Palestine, he placed Zedekiah on the throne of Judah after burning Jerusalem and carrying 4,600 of the leading and influential Jews into captivity. Upon arriving back in Babylon with his captives, the king ordered that certain young men be trained in the ways of Babylon. He gave them a daily provision of food and drink from the king's own table. Daniel, one of the Hebrew captives, was among the young men selected for this honor; however, he and his three friends requested a simple diet.

In Daniel 2 and 3 we read the account of the king and a dream he had that Daniel, through God's providence, told Nebuchadnezzar his dream when his magicians and astrologers could not do so. In the dream Nebuchadnezzar saw a giant statue whose head was made out of fine gold. Its breast and arms were of silver; its belly and thighs of brass; its legs of iron; and its feet part iron and part clay. Then a stone struck the feet of the statue and broke it into thousands of pieces. And the stone that hit the image became a great mountain and filled the whole earth.

God also showed Daniel the meaning of the dream. Each material represented a different kingdom that would overthrow the kingdom before it. The gold represented Rome; the silver, Medo-Persia; the brass, Greece; the iron, Rome; and the feet of iron and clay, Europe. Today the European nations feature a wide variety of religious and ethnic groups, consisting of Christians, Jews, Muslims, etc.

The stone represents the kingdom of God that will destroy all the kingdoms of the earth and stand forever.

In 587 BC Nebuchadnezzar returned to Judah because Zedekiah rebelled against him. Nebuchadnezzar laid siege to the city until Zedekiah surrendered. The king of Babylon then killed all of Zedekiah's sons in front of him before putting out Zedekiah's eyes and throwing him in prison where he stayed until his death (2 Kings 24, 25).

In 525 BC the Persians conquered Egypt. During Persian rule the Egyptians had some degree of independence. It was also at this time that the Jews were scattered to all parts of the known world. The last historical record of events in the order of time of the Old Testament was the book of Nehemiah, the Jewish cupbearer to Artaxerxes, king of Persia from 464-424 BC. This was about a century after the Persian King Cyrus allowed the Jews to return to their homeland from Babylonia captivity.

Alexander the Great (356-323 BC) conquered Egypt in 332 BC, and by the year 329 BC, the Greeks ruled most of Asia, which extended to the border of India. Alexander introduced Hellenism from Greek culture to all the conquered lands. Alexander, upon returning to Greece, made his general, Ptolemy, governor of Egypt. After Alexander's death, Ptolemy made himself king of Egypt, reigning from 323-285 BC. The Ptolemy dynasty continued from 323 BC to 30 BC, with Ptolemy XIII serving as the last member of the royal legacy.

During the Hellenistic rule, the Jews in Palestine were influenced by the Greek culture that surrounded them, and they adopted many Greek practices. As they lived and worked under the rule of four godless kings, religion became tainted by the seductive power of the paganism of Hellenism, the degenerated form of the Greek religion.

Baal was a fertility god among the ancient Semitic peoples, later a chief god. Also used to refer to a false god or idol. The Hebrews called Baal, Beelzebub. Baal is mentioned in the New Testament (Rom. 11:4). The New Testament refers to Baal as prince of the devils. For a description of Baal rites dating back to the ninth century BC, refer to the story of the prophet Elijah's showdown with the priests of Baal (I Kings 18:18-40). King Ahab and his wife, Jezebel, turned the worship of Baal into a degenerated practice of sensual pleasures.

There was a dramatic clash of the religious outlook of the Hebrew's God, Yahweh, and the Hellenistic god, Baal, which was known as the god of fertility. After the Jews settled down to a stable life, antagonisms diminished and a process of assimilation began. By degrees, loyalty to Yahweh wavered as Baal

14 The Bible Around and Beyond

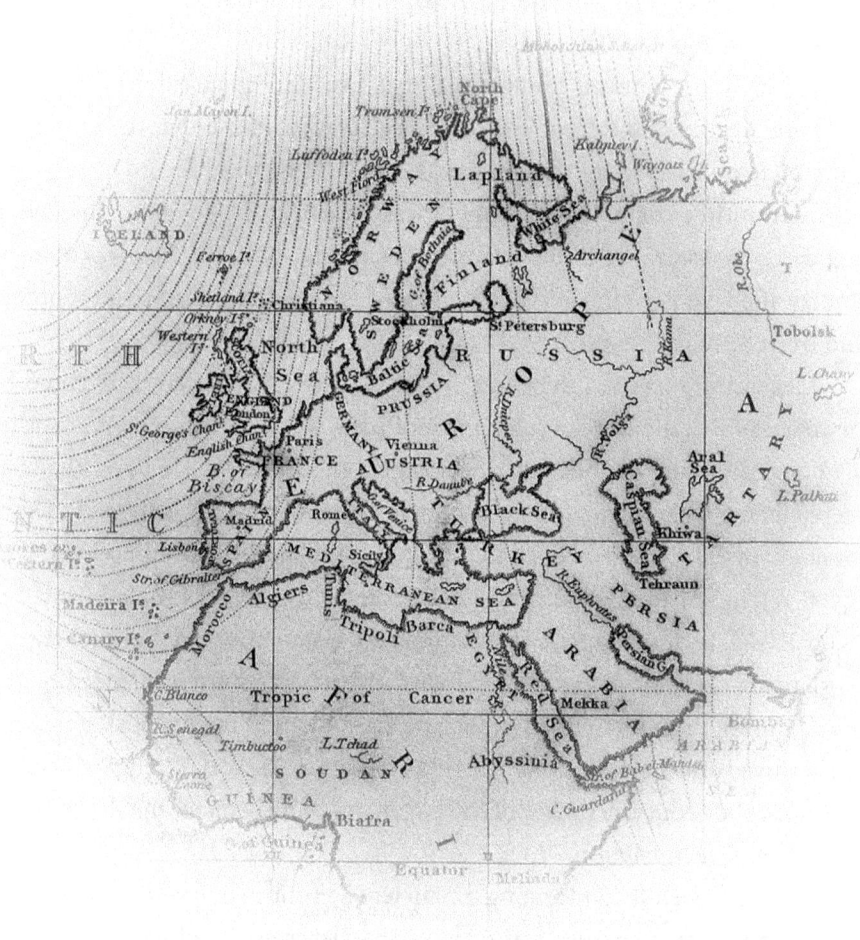

Map of Europe and the Middle East circa 1860

became more alluring. Idols, shrines, festivals, and habits all found their way into Hebrew life. Polytheism, belief in or worship of many gods, threatened to debilitate the Jews and engulf the world.

Sodom and Gomorrah

Sodom, a city destroyed by fire together with a neighboring city, Gomorrah, because of the sinfulness of the people.

Sodom, one of the cities at the southern end of the Dead Sea. The wickedness of its inhabitants was a proverbial enigmatical or perplexing adage in which a profound truth is cloaked or hidden in its meaning.

Sodom is a biblically used word signifying one possessed of the sin of Sodom. A Sodomite, a person or inhabitant of Sodom.

Lot, the son of Haran and Abraham's nephew took residence in Sodom, his sojourn, or short stay in Sodom is referred to in Genesis 19:12-17. God destroys the city, 19:24,25.

Matthew 10:15, Verily I say unto you, it shall be more tolerable for the land of Sodom and Gomorrah, in the day of Judgment than for that city.

Noah's Ark

After human beings had lived on earth for a time, God saw the wickedness, corruption, and evil of humanity, and God vowed to destroy evil (Gen. 6, 7).

Noah, who was tenth in descent from Adam, in the line of Seth, was a just man and perfect in his generation, for Noah walked with God. Noah found grace in the eyes of the Lord.

God told Noah to build an ark to escape the flood waters that He would send. He gave him directions on how to build it. The flood was to destroy the evil and wicked ways of earth's inhabitants.

The ark was to be made of gopher wood with rooms throughout the ark. Noah was to pitch it within and without. The length was to be 300 cubits, the breadth, fifty cubits, and the height, thirty cubits. The door of the ark was to be set in the side with lower, second, and third stories.

God instructed Noah to bring his wife and his three sons and their wives into the ark. Two of every living beast and fowl, male and female, was to find safety in the ark. Noah was also to store food from his garden for his family and food for the animals, in addition to seed to plant after the flood.

It came to pass that after all of God's instructions for the building of the ark were accomplished and Noah, his family, and the animals were safe in the ark that God shut the door of the ark. Seven days later rain began to fall, and it continued to fall for forty days and forty nights until water covered the earth. The ark floated on top of the floodwaters for 150 days until coming to rest upon Mt. Ararat, which is in eastern Turkey near the borders of Iran, Armenia, and Azerbaijan.

After the waters dried up from the earth, God told Noah, "Go forth of the ark, thou, and thy wife, and thy sons, and thy sons' wives with thee. Bring forth with thee every living thing that is with thee, of all flesh, both of fowl, and of cattle, and of every creeping thing that creepeth upon the earth; that they may breed abundantly in the earth, and be fruitful, and multiply upon the earth" (Gen. 8:16, 17).

Upon leaving the ark, Noah built an altar to God and offered burnt offerings on the altar, which God accepted and promised to never curse the earth again with a flood. "And God said, This is the token of the covenant which I make between me and you and every living creature that is with you, for perpetual generations: I do set my bow in the cloud, and it shall be for a token of a covenant between me and the earth. And it shall come to pass, when I bring a cloud over the earth, that the bow shall be seen in the cloud: And I will remember my covenant, which is between me and you and every living creature of all flesh; and the waters shall no more become a flood to destroy all flesh" (Gen. 9:12–15).

God's covenant is signified by the rainbow.

Chapter 2

Idol Worship and Ancient Gods

An idol is a material object that is worshipped as a god. It doesn't have any substance, but it can be seen because it is made out of wood or metal. Idolatry was widespread among primitive peoples of the world. It also entered into the practices and beliefs of more advanced peoples, such as the Egyptians, Greeks, and Romans.

Following are a listing of gods that have been worshipped throughout history:

- **Apollo:** The god of light and patron of the arts.
- **Ashtaroth:** A female goddess worshipped by Greek and Romans. Her symbol was the planet Venus.
- **Baal:** The chief male god of the Babylonians. The god of fertility. When the Israelites settled Canaan, Baal was worshipped by the people throughout the land. The Israelites later adopted worshipping Baal, but then condemned the practice.
- **Beelzebub:** The prince of the devils, second to Satan himself. A Philistine god.
- **Cupid:** The god of love.
- **Diana:** The temple of Diana was built around 350 BC and was the scene of orgies as well as worship.
- **Flora:** The goddess of flowers.
- **Golden calf:** Worshipped by the Israelites while Moses was on Mount Sinai.
- **Iris:** Goddess of the rainbow and messenger of the gods.
- **Jupiter:** The god who ruled over all other gods and all people.

- **Hebe:** The goddess of youth.
- **Mars:** The god of war.
- **Mercury:** Messenger of the gods. The god of commerce and travel.
- **Minerva:** The Roman goddess of wisdom, arts, and warfare. Depicted as wearing a helmet and shield. The spoils of war were dedicated to her. There were two temples set up in her honor in Rome.
- **Nemesis:** The goddess of vengeance who meted out punishment to evildoers and lawbreakers.
- **Neptune:** The god of the sea in Roman culture. Same as Poseidon in Grecian culture.
- **Odin:** The supreme god of the German tribes. The bestower of wisdom and valor. The Romans called this good Woden and honored him on Woden Day or Wednesday.
- **Olympus:** The abode of the gods.
- **Osiris:** An Egyptian god that was ruler of the underworld; the god of death and resurrection. Osiris became identified with numerous other gods, and his worship spread to Rome and Greece.
- **Pan:** The god of woods, fields, and shepherds. Represented as having two small horns and the lower limbs of a goat. He was very fond of music.
- **Pluto:** The god who rules over the lower world, Hades.
- **Priapus:** A Roman god of fertility.
- **Saturn:** The god of agriculture.
- **Satyr:** A Greek god that was said to be half man and half goat of a lustful nature (Lev. 17:7). Christian writers ranked the satyrs among demons and devils (Rev. 18:2).
- **Sol:** The sun god.
- **Uranus:** A Greek god and father of Titans, Furies, and Cyclopes.
- **Venus:** The goddess of love and beauty.
- **Vulcan:** The god of fire.
- **Zeus:** The greatest of the Greek gods. This god was identified with Jupiter of the Romans and the Ammon of Egypt.

The worship of the Babylonian gods and goddesses is said to have been carried on until the fourth century of the Christian era. One of the more dominant characteristics of the Babylonians was their reverence for their gods. The

Idol Worship and Ancient Gods   19

earliest historical period of Babylonia probably dates from about 3000 BC, and literary texts were rare before 2000 BC.

In the early Christian church very few sculptures were produced because statues were considered too closely connected with graven images, which the second commandment of the Bible forbids.

Statues of Zeus and Antiochus guarding tomb in Turkey

Greek churches permitted icons or pictures, but they disallowed graven images according to the second commandment (Exod. 20:4; Deut. 5:8). Eastern churches now use icons, which are not images in sculpture format but are a combination of the very flat relief with painting. The Lutheran Church still permits their moderate use. In Britain in the seventeenth century, iconoclast was reintroduced and many statues were destroyed.

The Persians (Iran) converted to Mohammadanism greatly against their will, and the Muslim religion forbade the use of human and animal figures in decorative art. Legalization of representational pictures by the Eastern Orthodox Church took place in 843.

The Roman Catholic Church strongly supports the use of images, which became crystal clear in the twenty-fifth session of the Council of Trent in Italy. At the same time, distinction was carefully drawn between *latreia*, or adoration, and *douleia*, or reverence. It was also taught that even reverence must not be paid to the picture or image but only to the persons so represented. The worship of images was the subject of heated controversy in the early church.

Aristotle was an outstanding Greek philosopher (384–322 BC) who was a student in Plato's Academy and also worked as a teacher. He concerned himself with life as it is, rather than with life as it ought to be, as Plato had done. The legacy of his thought dominated Mohammedan, Jewish, and Christian worlds for nearly 2,000 years.

Neo-Platonism is a doctrine founded upon Plato's metaphysical and ethical principles. They acquired a heavy religious tinge for they were the basis on which the last of the pagan thinkers hoped to raise a system to combat Christianity. Among the early Christian thinkers, these doctrines were widespread and served as the first basis for the growth of theology and scholastic philosophy. The most famous of the Christian Neo-Platonists was Saint Augustine, and the foundation of the synthesis between philosophy and Catholic theology.

Saint Augustine was born at Tagaste, now Algeria, in AD 354. Saint Augustine preached that everything God made is good. Evil is a corruption of nature brought about by the exercise of the human will and calamity and misfortune are necessary ingredients of human life. This concept can be traced back to Marcus Aurelius, emperor of Rome, the apostle Paul, and others. Saint Augustine died in AD 430.

Mythology

Every cultural group known in the history of humankind has developed a mythology so the myth-making faculty is a universal trite.

Mythologies are more easily described than defined, but in spite of many wide differences, they occupy a borderland area between religion and folklore.

Religion is formal, orthodox, ritualistic, whereas mythology embodies the stories about superhuman beings rather than the forms of their worship.

In example, most familiar to western civilization, mythology brings to mind the great Gracco-Roman and Norse Pantheons, a temple built by Agrippa in Rome in 27 BC for all gods, demigods, and heroes, which were highlighted by their individualized personalities and elaborately detailed adventures.

Primitive man vested rivers and mountains and crocodiles and serpents with mystic powers. In time he transferred his worship of the object itself to a life power, then to a personality clothes with that power. Zeus is first the sky, then a force within the sky, then a God with the sky power.

Gods

The ancient Greek gods exceeded men in beauty, strength, and power, but Zeus, the sky and father god; and Athena, the war goddess; Poseidon, the god of waters; Aphrodite, the goddess of love; and the other gods celebrated in literature and art, remain at all times human in form and emotion.

The Norse gods, likewise, reflect human behavior in a magnified way and rule over special natural range of influence.

Heroes

The hero in mythology is a being less than a god and more than a man. Sometimes he is a demigod, one of whose parents is a God.

The Geek heroes were often better known than their gods. The strength of Hercules, a son of Zeus, has made him the outstanding figure in Western mythology. The siege of Troy is dominated by the warrior Achilles, a strong and wise hero of that siege.

A brief description of the ancient gods, Greek and Roman: Jupiter, Minerva, Neptune, and Venus; the Norse gods: Odin, Thor, Tyr, Freyr, Balder, and Loki; the Greek heroes: Hercules, Achilles, Odysseus; the Irish hero: Cuchulainn; and the English hero: Arthur, can be found in Webster's dictionary.

Although there are some supernatural happenings, such as things appearing unexpectedly or in an extraordinary way; i.e., ghostly, pale, shadowy apparitions that are supposed to be the disembodied spirit of a deceased person or objects in a room moving about, or hearing knocking sounds, etc.

There are many speculations and theories concerning these phenomenon, but they are still scientifically unexplainable.

Chapter 3

The Building of the Roman Empire

The Romans have a long history. The Roman Kingdom was established in 753 BC and operated until 509 BC, at which time the monarchical form of government was overthrown and replaced with a republic.

The Roman Republic consisted of two consuls who were elected each year for a one-year term. The consuls ruled the land in the place of a king. The republic form of government lasted from 527–509 BC. It was then replaced with the Roman Empire, which was an autocratic form of government that lasted until AD 1453 then under the rulership of Constantine.

Rulers

Julius Caesar was born in 102 BC to a noble family. He was elected consul to the Senate in 59 BC. He was one of two chief magistrates; the other at the time was Pomprey, a Roman general. In time the Senate was shorn of a good deal of its importance and the power of rule fell to the chief magistrates.

Julius Caesar lived from 102–44 BC. He was a great Roman dictator. Some of his famous statements are "the die is cast" and "I came, I saw, I conquered." His wars were of military genius, as proved by an exact study of his campaigns with the unprecedented moderation and fairness he showed toward his opponents.

Julius Caesar with his legions, an ancient Roman army numbering from 3,000 to 6,000 men with 300 to 700 cavalry, subdued the whole of Gaul (France) in 58 BC, the Belgian tribes in 57 BC, and other tribes on the west coast of Europe. In 56 BC he defeated the invading German tribes, and one year later in 54 BC he invaded Britain and forced Cassivellaunus, a British chieftain, to pay tribute.

Julius Caesar then turned his attention to the east. From Egypt he and his troops marched through Syria and Asia Minor (Turkey) and returned to Rome in 47 BC as masters of the Roman world.

Herod the Great (74–4 BC) rose to power through the help of Julius Caesar, and he became king of Judea in 40 BC. This was after the Roman General Pompey captured the city of Jerusalem after a three-year siege. The Jews who escaped death were rushed to the slave markets or the East or to the gladiatorial arenas in the chief cities.

There is a discrepancy in the year of Herod the Great's death as he lived after Jesus was born. It was in the last year of his life that he ordered the massacre of all baby boys under two years of age living in Bethlehem. The birth of Jesus took place either in late 5 BC or early 4 BC, and it is said that Herod died in 4 BC.

After Herod's death, his son Antipas Herod ruled from 4 BC until Rome exiled him to Lyons, France, and then to Spain in AD 38. While king he imprisoned and executed John the Baptist. Herod Agrippa, grandson of Herod the Great, became king in AD 38. During his reign he had the apostle James executed and Peter imprisoned. He died in AD 44. Herod Agrippa, the son of Agrippa I, took the side of Rome when the Jews waged war in 67 AD. The total Herod dynasty lasted more than 100 years.

Ptolemy XIII was the king of Egypt around 43 BC and ruler of Palestine during the Hellenism period. The Pharisees accepted the new doctrine of resurrection and life after death during his reign. The eldest surviving daughter of Ptolemy Auletes, Cleopatra and her brother were placed on the throne of Egypt when their father died in 51 BC. When the victorious Julius Caesar arrived in Alexandria in 48 BC, her brother having been killed in battle, Caesar made Cleopatra queen of Egypt. Cleopatra bore

Statue of Julius Caesar at the Louvre

Caesar a son in 47 BC; then she followed him to Rome and was apparently there at the time of his death. Because of his power and influence, it made him an object of jealousy and suspicion by members of the Senate. He neglected warnings and was killed by members of the Senate in 44 BC.

Caesar was killed by the Senators of Rome for not rationalizing or conforming to reason of disbanding the Senate, which is The Supreme Council of the Roman Empire. This would make him Caesar, the sole Dictator, the Supreme ruler with absolute power and authority. This in the eyes of the full Senate, would be detrimental to the empire. It is noted that the Senate of Rome, whose membership and functions varied at different periods of Roman rule.

Returning to Egypt after Julius Caesar died, she assisted Emperor Augustus and Mark Antony, his army commander, in securing the domination of Egypt. With Antony she soon secured the same power she enjoyed with Julius Caesar.

Cleopatra and Antony's association and ambition led to war between Antony and Augustus. In the war, Cleopatra betrayed Antony and withdrew her ships from battle. Antony's army deserted him in the face of Augustus' greater army, and Antony killed himself by falling on his sword. Upon learning of Antony's death, Cleopatra was deathly afraid that Augustus would kill her, so she reportedly committed suicide by allowing a poisonous snake to bite her. Cleopatra died at the age of 39. Upon her death, Egypt became a province of Rome.

Augustus, successor to Julius Caesar, became the first emperor of the Roman Empire, ruling from 63 BC to AD 14, which was during a portion of Jesus' life. Augustus served in the Senate at the same time as Mark Antony. But when Augustus defeated Antony in the Battle of Actium, Antony committed suicide in 31 BC.

Weapons of War

Sword

A hand weapon having a long sharp pointed blade, usually with a sharp edge on one or both sides, set in a hilt. It was carried in a sheath girded to the loins, EXOD. 32:27; 2 SAM. 20:8, and was a symbol of War as the Plowshare was of Peace, ISA. 2:4; MIC. 4:3.

Spear, Lancet

A weapon consisting of a long wooden shaft with a sharp point usually of metal or stone, for thrusting or throwing.

Javelin,. a light spear with a pointed wooden or metal shaft, about 8 1/2 feet long, thrown for distance.

Bow and Arrow

An offensive weapon used in civilian as well as military life. It was made of strong elastic timber or other material, the two ends of which are partly bent toward each other an held by a string or cord which itself is thus stretched taut; the latter, a shaft, pointed or barbed at one end and notched and feathered at the other , which the bow is designed to propel with force.

The bow and arrow appeared during or before the beginning of the New Stone Age and were invented independently of each other by early man in different parts of the world. It made it possible for the savage to protect himself against wild animals and to kill them at a distance for food, and thus insured man's survival.

In later periods, the introduction of the bow and, arrow into warfare influenced the course of history.

Sling

An offensive weapon used by hunters, and shepherders against wild beasts, 1SAM.17:40 and in warfare, 2 KINGS 3:25. It consisted of a leather thong wider in the middle than at the ends. After placing a stone in the broad middle portion, the slinger grasped its two ends with one hand and swung it in a circle about his head. Upon releasing one end of the thong, the stone was sent hurtling toward its mark.

Dart

An offensive weapon, apparently a sort of arrow or light throwing spear, 2 SAM. 18:14. Also as a large arrows or bolts that might be ignited and hurled by a Catapult.

HEZEKIAH, King of Judah 726–697 B.C., made Darts and shields for the defence of Jerusalem, 2 CHRON. 32:5. Paul made reference to fiery Darts, JOB 41 :26; PROV. 7:2 3, EPH. 6:16 and HEB. 12:20.

Catapult

An ancient device for hurling projectiles, first used as an implement of war by the ancient Romans.

The larger kind was mounted on a strong wooden platform, the trigger or projector was drawn back by ropes, and then held by a catch, while the missile was placed on it prior to letting it fly.

By this means very heavy rocks were projected a considerable distance. The term "Catapult" is now applied to various devices for launching aircraft, rockets, etc., especially from ships.

Shield

A shield is a broad piece of protective armor carried in the hand or worn on the forearm to ward off blows or missiles.

Armor

Armor is a protection for the individual warrior, as existing from a remote period in history

Fragments of armor of overlapping scales of Bronze have been found in Egyptian graves dating from long before the Christian Era.

The armor of the Greeks centuries before Christ is well known. It was of Bronze, consisting of Helmet, Chest Protection, Shin guards, and Shield.

Roman armor is also familiar, especially from the reliefs on Trajan's Columns; Trajan, Marcus, A.D. 53–117 born in Spain, he was the first Roman Emperor not of Italian birth.

The Armor used iron as well as bronze. Characteristic are the overlapping strips over the shoulders and around the body and the deeply curved rectangular shields.

War

War is an armed conflict. Early wars were little more than a skirmish between opposing sides, usually of few men each.

From the time of Saul, the menace of the Philistines and other foes necessitated a standing army. Tactics were simple.

The force was divided, sometimes into two companies, sometimes three, ambush and night attacks were common.

The Trumpet gave the signal to open and cease battle. Fighting was done chiefly by Spearmen, Bowmen, and Swordsmen.

Horses and Chariots were subjected to Siege. Assaults were made by Battering Rams and Catapults.

Siege; the encirclement of a fortified place by an opposing armed force intending to take it, usually by blockade and bombardment.

Airplane

Many Bible passages are strikingly descriptive of aircraft. Likening the means of a city's defence to "'Birds Flying" (ISA. 31:5) suggests a formation of circling warplanes. Jeremiah predicted that the military might of Chaldea "shall fly as an Eagle" and that it shall spread its wings over Moab, a land to be invaded (JER. 48:40, 41; compare HAB. 1:8. Ezekiel's description of those guardian creatures the Cherubim, is surprisingly like that of the protecting aircraft of an army. The prophet "Heard the noise of their wings like the noise of great waters", like thunder, and like the "noise of an HOST." Battleplane formation could scarcely be more vividly described than in Ezekiel's words; "under the firmament were their wings straight, the one toward the other", EZEK. 1:23,24).

Roman Infrastructure and Domination

Whatever term is used to describe the Roman government, the key position of the government was to subdue the world and bring people under its control. Following are dates of Rome's conquests:

- Greece (Macedonia) – 197 BC
- North Africa, invaded Carthage near Tunisia – 146 BC
- Syria and Palestine annexed to Rome – 64 BC
- Gual, which included northern Italy, France, Belgium, and Germany – 58–56 BC
- Britain – 54 BC
- Egypt – 47 BC
- Turkey – 45 BC
- Spain – 44 BC
- Morocco – 42 BC

The Building of the Roman Empire

All roads led to Rome from the fifth century BC to Rome's greatest expansion in AD 117. These roads were built mainly be tens of thousands of slaves, and coupled with the sea lanes, the roads facilitated travel between nations within the Roman Empire.

During the reign of the Roman Empire, they operated more than 62,000 miles of roads that were graded and gravel-paved. At fifteen feet wide, they were kept well maintained. There were stops at set intervals where travelers could water their horses, repair their chariots, rest for the night, and/or purchase food.

The roads extended from Asia Minor, a peninsula in west Asia between the Black and Mediterranean seas, including most of Turkey, to the Iberian peninsula, an ancient name for the region that is now Spain and Portugal. It is also an ancient Greek name of Spain.

On conquering a city or nation, Caesar incorporated the conquered army into his legions. Under Roman supervision he gave them control of their country to stop acts of rebellion, looting, and criminal conduct. With a period of just and wise administration Roman rule ensured prosperity and peace to the country.

Upon the death of Caesar Augustus, Claudius Tiberius became emperor of Rome. It was during his reign that the trial and execution of Jesus took place. He reigned from 42 BC to AD 37.

However, Rome did not stand for disobedience from its subjects, which is what caused problems for the Christians. In AD 44 Emperor Claudius Tiberius issued an edict, an authoritative proclamation, expelling all the Christian leaders from Rome. Many sought sanctuary in Britain, including Peter.

When Rome conquered a new city, they would go about constructing buildings and other structures. In this way, it was unmistakable what cities were under Roman rule. The materials they used and the style of the architecture was definitely Roman. They used wood, stone, brick, and concrete in their buildings. The Romans discovered that they could make concrete by mixing clean sand with lime and small stones. Stucco, marble, and alabaster were used as surfacing materials of rough work.

For example when Emperor Hadrian toured to the edge of the known world, Britain, in AD 122, he gave orders to his men to construct one of the most formidable building projects the world had ever seen—a wall fifteen feet high and up to ten feet thick stretching eighty-five miles, from sea to sea. Hadrian ordered the building to separate the Roman citizens and other cosmopolitan residents from across the Roman Empire from barbarians, anyone who was not a part of the Roman Empire. Besides the massive wall, extensive pits and ditches ten feet deep and twenty feet across were constructed. Gates appeared at regular intervals along the wall.

Frontiers built like this were not primarily for defense against attacks, but they were more about controlling the movement of people. Emperor Severus later extended and strengthened the wall with many more forts in AD 209.

The Romans gleaned useful natural material, besides spiritual and intellectual matter in their occupation of countries that would be beneficial to all the nations of the Empire.

The dispersing of this information increased the prestige of the Romans and solidified their bond of annexed nations.

Roman Numerals

The Roman Empire also gave the world the early numbering system. Before the introduction of Roman numerals, people represented numbers by notches on a stick by making perpendicular strokes. These strokes were the primary element within the earliest Egyptian, Semitic, Indian, and Roman cultures, but there was no zero. In the Roman system a symbol preceding a symbol for a larger number is subtracted from the latter. Thus IX is 9, and XI is 11.

The basic symbols are I=1; V=5; X=10; L=50; C=100; D=500; and M=1000. This system was used by the Babylonians, Greeks, and Romans were quite adequate for recording numbers, even large ones, but it was entirely inadequate for arithmetic calculations.

Thus the early number system had no symbol for zero until the so-called Hindu-Arabic decimal system, which came about probably during the eighth century. The concept of zero was fully developed by AD 130.

Calendar

This section addresses the day of the week Christians make their chief day of rest and religious observance. Most Christian church denominations make Sunday, the first day of the week, their chief day of rest and worship.

Two Christian denominations, Seventh-day Adventists and Seventh Day Baptists, are distinct groups who hold that the Old Testament and Christ sanctioned Sabbath observance on the seventh day of the week, which is, as we know it now as Saturday.

Sabbath

The Sabbath, the day on which the fourth commandment enjoins abstention from work of all kinds, is the Jewish seventh day of the Jewish week. No ancient Hebrew law made it a day of worship.

This feature came in with the synagogue after the exile. Jewish Christians in New Testament times observed the Sabbath. The term "Sabbath" applied to Sunday is a misnomer (a misapplied name or designation, an error in naming a person or thing), which dates from the early part of the seventeenth century and gave rise to the Puritan custom and laws enforcing a strict Sabbathlike observance of Sunday.

Much later arose the existing denominations that hold that the observance of the seventh day is a perpetual divine command.

The fourth commandment states: "Remember the sabbath day, to keep it holy.... For in six days the Lord made heaven and earth, the sea, and all that in them is, and rested the seventh day: wherefore the Lord blessed the sabbath day, and hallowed it."

Again, the term Sabbath applied to Sunday is a misnomer. The Lord rested on the seventh day, the Sabbath, a day of rest and meditation.

To further explain this misconception, go to the word "calendar" in the Encyclopedia. Note the time or date of the early calendar: year, season, months, days, and naming of the days of the week. Keep in mind that God the Father rested on the seventh day before man created his calendar.

Early Calendars

A calendar is a device resulting from historic and present-day methods of dividing time into an orderly arrangement of periods.

Egypt had a calendar in 4241 BC. It had 365 day, twelve 30-day months, plus five feast days.

The early Babylonians had a twelve 30-day month, but it was nearly five and one quarter days too short.

The Greek calendar had a 354-day year in the fifth century BC.

The early Roman calendar was a whole season out of step.

In 45 BC the Julian calendar by Julius Caesar, put into effect a year before his assassination, had 365 ½ days, some of the names of the months we have today.

The Gregorian calendar by Pope Gregory XIII is now fully established in all Western nations except the Greek who go by their calendar of AD 1582. A Jesuit priest revised the Julian calendar for the pope.

The Mohammedan calendar, which was instituted in AD 631, is in use in Turkey, Arabia, Persia, India, Egypt, and parts of Africa and the Far East. It is an obstacle to worldwide calendar reform, which is in consideration today. It is a very interesting topic that looks promising. For more information look up "calendar" in the encyclopedia.

The early Roman calendar of 45 BC named the twelve lunar months, some surviving to this day: Martius, Aprilis, Maius, Junius, Quintilis, Sextilis, September, October, November, December, Januarius, and Februarius. The month of Quintilis was later changed to Julius in honor of Caesar. Augustus Caesar changed the name of the month Sextilis to Augustus in honor of himself.

Days of the Week

From the Saxon designation of the planets (among which the ancients included the sun and moon) have been formed the modern names of the days of the week: Saturday (Saturn or Saterdaeg), Sunday (sun or Sonnam); Monday (moon or Monam); Tuesday (Mars or Tiu, Tives); Wednesday (Mercury or Woden); Thursday (Jupiter or Thors); and Friday (Venus or Frigas).

"But, beloved, be not ignorant of this one thing, that one day is with the Lord as a thousand years, and a thousand years as one day" (2 Peter 3:8).

"Thus the heavens and the earth were finished, and all the host of them. And on the seventh day God ended his work which he had made; and he rested on the seventh day from all his work which he had made. And God blessed the seventh day, and sanctified it: because that in it he had rested from all his work which God created and made" (Gen. 2:1–3).

Time is the indefinite, unlimited duration in which things are considered as happening in the past, present, or future, every moment there has ever been or ever will be.

The days are a period of light between sunrise and sunset. The time (twenty-four hours) that it takes the earth to revolve once on its axis marks each day.

The calendar is divided into twelve months. The period of a complete revolution of the moon with reference to some fixed point. And a year is a period of 365 days (366) divided into twelve months. Any of the four arbitrary divisions of the year are known as seasons; chiefly spring, summer, fall, or winter.

The Julian Calendar

The calendar is the device resulting from historic and present day methods of dividing time into an orderly arrangement of periods. The early Egyptians had the most exact and complex calendar believed to date from 4241 BC.

The Julian calendar, based on the year length of 365 ½ days, an intercalary day was added every fourth year (the origin of leap year), and the year was divided into twelve months of unequal length because 365 is not divisible by twelve.

The last six names of the months are merely the number of the months in the list: sixth, seventh, etc.

- January (Januarius) – Roman God Janus, over doors and gateways
- February (Sabine, people of ancient Italy) – Word for cleanliness
- March (Martius) – Mars, god of war
- April (Aperire) – Latin name meaning to open, buds of spring
- May (Maia) – Mother of the god Mercury
- June (Juno) – Sister and wife of Jupiter
- July (Quintillis) – For Julius Caesar, 102–44 BC
- August (Sextilis) – For Augustus Caesar, 63 BC–AD 14
- September – Was Latin for nine
- October – Was Latin for ten
- November – Was Latin for eleven
- December – Was Latin for twelve

The weekday is not based on any periodicity in nature as are day, month, and year. The arrangement of the heavenly bodies according to their distances from earth was in the order Saturn (the most distant), Jupiter, Mara, the sun, Venus, Mercury, and the Moon. The modern name of the days of the week: Saturday (Saturn), Sunday (Sun), Monday (Moon), Tuesday (Mars), Wednesday (Mercury), Thursday (Jupiter), and Friday (Venus).

Time

The length of the solar day is the interval between sunrise and sunset. It varies with latitude; astronomical latitude, the angle between the direction of gravity; and the celestial latitude, the angular distance from a heavenly body.

The solar day encompasses the interval of time required for the earth to make a complete rotation on its axis around the sun. The "mean" solar day (the middle or intermediate position as to place and time; halfway between extremes) begins at midnight and is divided into twenty-four mean solar hours, and each hour is subdivided into mean solar minutes and seconds.

The earliest timepiece was a sundial. It is an instrument of great antiquity for measuring time by means of the motion of the sun's shadow cast by a rod on the sundial's surface onto numbers marking each hour. The time is crudely determined by the length of the sun's shadow, but it was a start.

Some mechanical clocks were constructed by the year 1400, but accuracy was very poor. No significant advance in timekeeping was made until about 1658 when the pendulum was applied to clocks.

In the next century the hairspring balance was applied to watches and clocks. By the year 1800 the accuracy of these timepieces, which were designed to keep uniform time, was sufficiently high to bring mean time into civil use. Mean solar time is time measured by the sun and having exactly equal divisions.

To avoid inconveniences in the world, standard time was introduced in 1883. This standard was located on the Prime Meridian, which from longitude is measured both east to west. Zero longitude passes through Greenwich, England, and is used as the basis for mean time throughout most of the world. The world as we know it today is divided into twenty-four zones, and all places, in any time zone, keep Greenwich Mean Time.

The time zone boundaries are not always straight lines. Most lines zigzag so as to eliminate inconvenient time changes when traveling. In some cases, cities and large areas have placed themselves in zones east of the ones in which they would naturally fall. There are four time zones in the United States: Eastern, Central, Mountain, and Pacific.

The civil day begins at midnight and is divided into two parts—a.m. (ante meridiem) and p.m. (post meridiem)—with each part divided into twelve hours.

Daylight savings time was introduced around 1918. During the summer months the clock is set ahead one hour. The rationale is that this gives more light for outdoor activities, which most people want to engage in during the warmer summer months.

Time is based on the earth's rotation in relation to the sun. The motion of the moon about the earth and of the planets in the solar system may also be used as independent methods of determining time. Careful observation of these bodies indicate that the earth's rotation speed alternately increases and decreases in an irregular manner. The changes in the length of the day are of the order of one or two thousandths of a second. Such changes are too small to detect with certainty with even the best clocks available. Hence, although it is unlikely that the mean solar second can remain absolutely constant, it may be regarded as such for the present.

Roman Sea Power

The Roman Empire led a mighty force of soldiers on foot and on the open waters. In the Middle Ages the galley was the warship and merchant ship of the Mediterranean Sea. It was a long narrow ship with one deck that could carry several hundred men. Propelled by twenty to thirty oars on both sides of the ship, powered by men sitting below the main deck. The rowers were usually prisoners and convicts chained to their oar.

A ship is a craft designed and built to be used in water transportation, propelled in ancient times by oars or sail. A ship is larger than a boat but the two renderings are some times used in interchangeably, as in John 6:17,19,21,23.

Paul in order to spread the gospel of Jesus Christ frequently crossed the Aegean Sea; the northeast division of the Mediterranean Sea, lying between Greece and Turkey. From Athens, Paul then made longer voyages to the City Of Puteoli; (Pozzuoli), which was made a province of Rome in 194 B.C., it contained a large cement plant, also blast furnaces and smelters. Near the city is an arms factory and naval shipbuilding yards.

36 The Bible Around and Beyond

Ancient Roman warship

Paul describes in detail, giving valuable information about the ships of his day, Acts 27:1–28:13.

Roman law and order made seaborne trade and travel relatively safe and contributed to the over-all development of international trade.

In those days, military service was often forced. In Britain, impressment was used regularly, especially for the navy. Naval officers bearing press warrants issued by the Admiralty would forcibly seize able-bodied men on the streets and in the taverns. Certain classes were exempt, such as married men, especially if they had children. Most of the men were vagabonds, tramps, paupers, and criminals.

It turned out that the impressed seamen were often mutinous, disloyal, or even dangerous. As a result of the poor quality of soldiers and seamen, the British began a type of Marines, a special force of naval personnel, formed and trained to police the large battle ships of the fleet and protect the ship's officers from the conscripted seamen. No British warship left port unless fully manned.

Games

Any form of play that is of a recreational nature is considered a game. Games in ancient Rome, however, seemed to be anything *but* play. Roman games often featured a gladiator who fought another person or animal with a sword of other weapon in an arena for the entertainment of spectators.

Gladiators were slaves, captives, or paid performers. One attraction featured two gladiators bravely fighting to the death, the winner gaining glory and gold while the loser died in the arena.

The Circus Maximus was built specifically for horse and chariot races and could accommodate 150,000 people. Emperor Vespasian commissioned construction of the Colosseum of Rome on the site of Nero's palace; the building was completed by Titus in AD 82. The Colosseum could seat 50,000 spectators. Underneath the arena were dens for wild animals and appliances for raising them to the arena floor. The corridors and inner walls were of stone and concrete and featured vaulted archways and ceilings.

These extravagant or spectacular shows often also featured the execution of Christians and criminals. Half starved wild animals were let loose in the arena with the person or persons who were condemned to die. These events were cruel and inhuman, but they drew thousands of spectators. The money derived from these events swelled the emperors coffers.

Ruins of the Collosseum in Rome

Roman Decline

The decline of the Roman Empire was gradual and was aggravated by constant plagues, natural and manmade, and famine. At this point there was a series of barbarian invasions. The armies of the Huns, led by Attila, invaded Persia in AD 446, terrorized Syria, and threatened Italy. The Huns were excellent horsemen and archers, and they could move with marvelous swiftness. They were capable of enduring hardship, and they were both brave and cruel at the same time. Their horse trappings, swords, and even their shoes were studded with gold and precious stones. Their tables, plates, goblets, and vases were gold and silver, which were fashioned by Grecian artists.

During this time Attila continued his relentless pursuit of Roman territory. It took the combined armies of the Romans and Visigoths to defeat Attila in a great battle just east of Paris. But these great armies did not follow up on their victory, and Attila turned to northern Italy where he plundered and devastated many cities before his sudden death in AD 453.

Although they had been their ally against the Huns, the Visigoths, a west Germanic people, invaded and conquered most of the Roman Empire in the third, fourth, and fifth centuries. The Visigoths took possession of Italy in AD 455.

In AD 451 the Council of Chalcedon met and recognized Constantinople as the capital of the Roman Empire. It was at this time that the Western Empire and Eastern Empire came together under one emperor.

In AD 476 the Western Empire of Rome had shrunk to Italy, Sicily, and Sardinia, islands off the coast of Italy. Twenty years later in AD 496 the Roman Catholic Church began its conquest of the barbarian world.

The Saxons, a Germanic people, raided the coasts of the North Sea. They were subdued by Charlemagne in the eighth century and became Christians through the conquest. Witikind, their leader, professed Christianity around AD 785.

Almost 300 years went by before Charlemagne, Charles the Great, became king of the Franks in AD 768 and became the power behind Western Europe, bringing Germany finally into the circle of European civilization. The Franks were a confederation of Germanic tribes. They became the leading military and political agent of Gaul, which is now France. On Christmas in AD 800, Pope Leo III crowned Charlemagne emperor of Rome.

The Viking Age

The Roman Empire ruled the world for an extended period of time, but there were other groups of people who were strong and had fortitude. In the eighth century the Vikings, a Scandinavian people group from Norway, Denmark, and Sweden, began a 300-year campaign of pillage and piracy throughout Europe. The Vikings on a grand scale, through threats of military assault, extorted great quantities of silver from England and other venerable western European states.

During the Viking age the Scandinavians were the best sailors and shipbuilders in the world.

"The remains of an ancient Viking warship, shows the timbers of the ship to be 121 feet bow to stern, and was capable of carrying 100 troops. The long narrow ships allowed the Vikings to enter countries through rivers, and this access enabled them to make lightning attacks on unsuspecting coastal hamlets and plunder parts of three continents."

Not being afraid of the ocean, they ventured farther and farther out on the sea. They could carry thousands of fighting men in their fleet of ships. To die in battle was to enter the Great Hall where Odin, the god of war and the dead, would greet them and they would receive their reward for bravely falling in battle.

The Vikings came to England after the Roman Empire had slightly weakened. The first recorded attack was in 793. Another more prolonged attack, with some limited occupation, took place in 856.

In France Charles III, also known as the Simple, concluded a peace treaty with Rollo, a Norse chieftain in 911 by ceding the lower valley of the Seine, Normandy, as a hereditary dukedom to him. Charles also induced Rollo to embrace Christianity, and he became a generous patron of the church.

The history of Viking exploits may be divided into two periods, one of plundering, which lasted into the tenth century, and the other as conquering invaders setting up kingdoms.

Eric the Red, a Norseman, discovered Vinland, now called Greenland in approximately 1000. A few years later his son Leif Ericsson, with an expedition of 160 men, colonized Greenland.

In a totally different geographic location, the Aztec people of Mexico enjoyed an advanced civilization before the conquest of Mexico by Cortes in

1519. The Aztec nation was a powerful and cultured people group who dominated Mexico at the time of the Spanish conquest. Their language was a mixture of Nahuatl, the Uto-Aztecan language of the tribes in Mexico during that time. This language is still spoken today by groups of people native to southern Mexico and Central America.

The Aztec's had a well-developed culture based on agriculture. They made pottery of excellent quality. They were beginning to cast metal, but most of their tools were still of stone, bone, and wood.

The pagans offered human sacrifices to propitiate, to obtain, the good will or appease their cruel and blood thirsty gods (2 Kings 16:3; 2 Chron. 28:3; Jer. 7:31).

In 1519 Cortes, with upwards of 400 men and a number of horses and cannons, invaded Mexico and established Spanish sovereignty. It was then that the Spanish influx began. Then in the spring of 1521, after frightful destruction and slaughter, he gained possession of the city of Mexico, and the Aztec Empire came to an end. Today the influence of Spain is evident in the architecture and religion, Roman Catholicism, in Mexico.

Cortes returned to Spain in 1540, and he died a few years later. He was buried in Seville; however, his remains were later taken to Mexico. Mexican historians discovered his bones in the wall of the Hospital of Jesus in Mexico City.

The Building of the Roman Empire   41

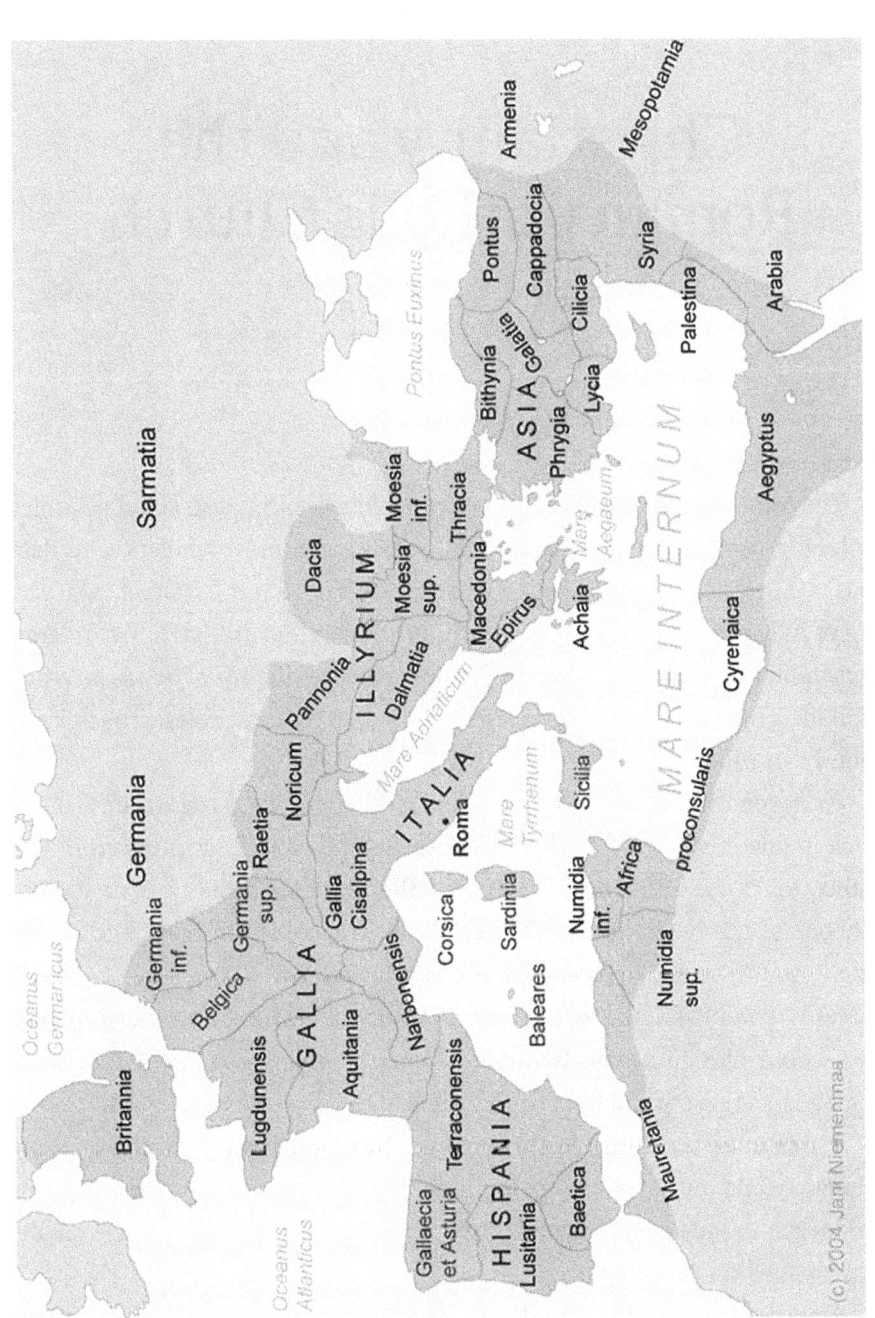

The Roman Empire

Chapter 4

Christianity and the Roman Catholic Church

Jesus

The Messiah was born in the town of Bethlehem in Judea, about six miles south of Jerusalem, between 6 and 4 BC according to most scholars. This date is based on the relation of Jesus' birth to the death of Herod the Great, who was king of Judea at the time of Jesus' birth. Just before his death, Herod ordered the slaughter of all male children in Bethlehem under the age of two in an effort to kill the King of the Jews. Herod died in 4 BC, so that places Jesus' birth right around that timeframe.

Jesus spent most of his growing up years living in Nazareth in Galilee, which is sheltered among rocky hills. Jesus learned about scripture from His mother, Mary. He also worked with his father, Joseph, in the carpentry shop. Only one of His boyhood experiences has been recorded in the Bible, that of His visit to the temple in Jerusalem at the age of twelve.

Jesus' parents knew, through the prophecy of Simeon, the great role that Jesus would play in saving humanity. However, many wonder if they fully grasped His ministry and the fact that He had to die to save the world.

It was after Jesus turned thirty that He started His ministry as devote Hebrews would not listen to even their rabbis if they were under that age. Jesus' work began in Judea, but He made trips to Galilee and Jerusalem as He taught the people who followed Him.

Samaria is a city in Palestine that became one of the foremost pagan centers in the East. The Samaritans mixed their religious beliefs between Jehovah and Baal. Most travelers avoided going through the city by going around it. The

Jews shunned the city and its inhabitants. However, on one trip Jesus stopped in Samaria on His way to Galilee. It was there that He sat at Jacob's well and spoke to the Samaritan woman and revealed to her, her sins and offered her Living Water. She ran into the city and told the people that there was a prophet at the well. Jesus stayed in Samaria two days teaching the people.

Jesus declared that He was anointed to preach the gospel to the poor. He performed many miracles of healing. More profound miracles included raising Jairus' daughter from the dead, feeding 5,000 people, and walking on water.

Jesus spoke in parables to the people. A parable is a comparison, a short simple story from which a moral or religious lesson may be drawn. A story in which people, things, and happenings have a hidden or symbolic meaning designed to convey some truth or moral lesson. A brief narrative or allegory founded on real scenes or events that has a religious application. Many parables suggest similarities that appear to exist between the natural and spiritual worlds. Jesus used parables to teach the people about nature and the natural laws of the kingdom of God. Documented in the Bible are thirty to forty of Jesus' parables.

The Sea of Galilee was in the northern section of the three provinces of Palestine west of the Jordan. This was the native territory of Jesus Christ, and the birthplace of all the apostles except Judas. Galilee was known for its great fertility. The water of the Sea of Galilee is pure and sweet. The Jordan River forms the main inlet and is the outlet for it.

Jesus chose twelve disciples to assist Him in His ministry. Many of His disciples were fishermen. At one point during His ministry, Jesus and His disciples withdrew from Galilee and headed north to the cities of Capernaum, Tyre, Sidon, and Decapolis. His purpose was primarily that of preparing His disciples for His approaching death and resurrection.

Jesus spent approximately three years with His small band of followers preaching the gospel of God. During this time, Jesus and His disciples incurred the active hostility of the priests, scribes, and Pharisees. The Roman authorities also became suspicious of Him after the title King of the Jews was ascribed to Him. For these reasons, Jesus was arrested and tried. He was first tried by the Jewish authorities, but because the death sentence could only be delivered by the Roman authorities, Jesus was brought before Pontius Pilate, the Roman procurator of Judea.

It was while Jesus was being tried by the Jewish authorities that Peter, one of Jesus' loyal disciples, watched the proceedings with fear and trepidation. When a maid identified Peter as a disciple of Jesus, Peter denied the claim. Three times he was identified as a follower, and three times he denied that he even knew Jesus (Matt. 26:69–75). It was then that Christ's prophecy came true that Peter would deny his Lord.

At Jesus' hearing, Pilate, who served as procurator of Judea during the ministries of John the Baptist and Jesus from AD 26–36, found no fault in Him, and he thought to scold Him sharply and then release Him. However, the mob cried, "Crucify Him; crucify Him." Pilate then offered to give them a prisoner named Barabbas, who was sentenced to death for sedition, rebellion against the government, and murder. The mob, instigated by the priests and Jewish authorities, cried, "Give us Barabbas; crucify Jesus." In order to pacify the mob, Pilate turned Jesus over to the high priests and Jewish officials for execution.

A Pharisee and member of the Sanhedrin, the Jewish court that possessed religious, civil, and criminal jurisdiction, Nicodemus was so impressed by Jesus' miracles that he obtained a secret interview with Jesus by night (John 3:1–13). He contributed myrrh, a perfume used in burial, toward the preparation of Jesus' body for burial.

"And one of the malefactors which were hanged railed on him, saying, If thou be Christ, save thyself and us. But the other answering rebuked him, saying, Dost not thou fear God, seeing thou art in the same condemnation? And we indeed justly; for we receive the due reward of our deeds: but this man hath done nothing amiss. And he said unto Jesus, Lord, remember me when thou comest into thy kingdom. And Jesus said unto him, Verily I say unto thee, Today shalt thou be with me in paradise" (Luke 23:39–43).

"Then saith he to the disciple, Behold thy mother! And from that hour that disciple took her unto his own home. After this, Jesus knowing that all things were now accomplished, that the scripture might be fulfilled, saith, I thirst. Now there was set a vessel full of vinegar: and they filled a spunge with vinegar, and put it upon hyssop, and put it to his mouth. When Jesus therefore had received the vinegar, he said, It is finished: and he bowed his head, and gave up the ghost" (John 19:27–30).

Jesus was crucified, but as He had foretold to His disciples, He was resurrected on the third day. Jesus had said, "Destroy this temple, and in three days I will raise it up.... But he spake of the temple of his body" (John 2:19, 21).

Christ's resurrection was declared by an angel to Mary Magdalene and the other Mary. The angel told them, "Fear not ye: for I know that ye seek Jesus, which was crucified. He is not here: for he is risen, as he said. Come, see the place where the Lord lay. And go quickly, and tell his disciples that he is risen from the dead; and, behold, he goeth before you into Galilee; there shall ye see him: lo, I have told you" (Matt. 28:1–8).

"And she went and told them that had been with him, as they mourned and wept. And they, when they had heard that he was alive, and had been seen of her, believed not" (Mark 16:10, 11).

Jesus appeared to His disciples after His resurrection and removed their unbelief. "And he said unto them, These are the words which I spake unto you, while I was yet with you, that all things must be fulfilled, which were written in the law of Moses, and in the prophets, and in the psalms, concerning me.... And said unto them, Thus it is written, and thus it behooved Christ to suffer, and to rise from the dead the third day" (Luke 24:44, 46).

The disciples later saw Him themselves on a number of different occasions. With the good news of His resurrection and the free gift of salvation, Jesus commissioned His disciples to spread the good news to the whole world.

Christianity is the teachings of Jesus Christ. The Christian faith is a unique link between God and humanity. From the standpoint of scientific observation and analysis, it must be viewed as one of the world's greatest religions.

If the evidence, when critically examined, sets one religion apart from others as of a different order, the conclusion is that its weight is proportionate to the evidence. Christians believe that rational evidence sustains such a claim for Christianity.

A Christian is a follower of Christ, a name first applied to the disciples at Antioch in Syria around AD 43, thus during the Apostolic Age, which ended with the death of John the Revelator. Although the history relating to his death is obscure, it is said that he preached for sixty-eight years after Jesus' resurrection.

After a time, three great divisions came out of Christianity: the Roman Catholic Church, Eastern Orthodox, and Protestantism. The Roman Empire officially recognized Christianity in AD 313 by Emperor Constantine. Pope Leo III crowned Charlemagne as holy Roman emperor in AD 800.

The following verses speak to the ministry of Jesus as taught by the apostles and the early Christian church after Jesus' resurrection.

- Acts 2:31—"He seeing this before spake of the resurrection of Christ, that his soul was not left in hell, neither his flesh did see corruption."
- Acts 26:23—"That Christ should suffer, and that he should be the first that should rise from the dead, and should shew light unto the people, and to the Gentiles."
- Romans 14:9—"For to this end Christ both died, and rose, and revived, that he might be Lord both of the dead and living."
- Galatians 2:16, 21—"Knowing that a man is not justified by the works of the law, but by the faith of Jesus Christ, even we have believed in Jesus Christ, that we might be justified by the faith of Christ, and not by the works of the law: for by the works of the law shall no flesh be justified.... I do not frustrate the grace of God: for if righteousness come by the law, then Christ is dead in vain."
- Hebrews 2:9—"But we see Jesus, who was made a little lower than the angels for the suffering of death, crowned with glory and honour; that he by the grace of God should taste death for every man."
- Hebrews 7:25—"Wherefore he is able also to save them to the uttermost that come unto God by him, seeing he ever liveth to make intercession for them."
- Hebrews 9:12—"Neither by the blood of goats and calves, but by his own blood he entered in once into the holy place, having obtained eternal redemption for us."
- 1 Corinthians 15:20-26—"But now is Christ risen from the dead, and become the firstfruits of them that slept. For since by man came death, by man came also the resurrection of the dead. For as in Adam all die, even so in Christ shall all be made alive. But every man in his own order: Christ the firstfruits; afterward they that are Christ's at his coming.... The last enemy that shall be destroyed is death."
- 2 Corinthians 5:21—"For he hath made him to be sin for us, who knew no sin; that we might be made the righteousness of God in him."
- 1 Timothy 1:8, 9—"But we know that the law is good, if a man use it lawfully; Knowing this, that the law is not made for a righteous man,

but for the lawless and disobedient, for the ungodly and for sinners, for unholy and profane."

The Twelve Disciples, Apostles

When Jesus began His ministry on earth, He selected twelve men to assist Him in preaching the gospel: Simon Peter, Andrew, James the son of Zebedee, John, Philip, Bartholomew, Thomas, Matthew, James the son of Alphaeus, Thaddaeus, Simon the Zealot, and Judas Iscariot.

The apostles were dignified writers and persuasive speakers because of the power of the Holy Spirit. The New Testament contains thirteen letters or epistles by the apostle Paul, three by the apostle John, two by Peter, and one each by James and Jude, brothers of Jesus Christ.

The apostles were clearly called by God. Jesus prayed for them and encouraged them. Not only did the apostles write and speak for God, but they also performed miracles in His name. Following are examples of God's calling and the work of the apostles.

- Matthew 10:1-8—Jesus gave the disciples power to cast out unclean spirits, to heal the sick, raise the dead, and cleanse the lepers.
- John 14:26 - "But the Comforter, which is the Holy Ghost, whom the Father will send in my name, he shall teach you all things, and bring all things to your remembrance, whatsoever I have said unto you."
- Acts 1:2-8 - Christ prepared His apostles for the coming of the Holy Spirit by telling them that the Comforter would come. This promise was fulfilled in these verses.
- Acts 2:7, 8 - "And they were all amazed and marvelled, saying one to another, Behold, are not all these which speak Galilaeans? And how hear we every man in our own tongue, wherein we were born?"
- Acts 5:12-16 - It is recorded that the apostles performed many miracles. They healed the sick and cast out demons, all in the name of Jesus Christ.
- Acts 9:33, 34 - Peter heals Aeneas of palsy.

Baptism is a ceremonial immersion in water or an application of water as a symbol of washing away sin and being spiritually purified. In the Bible the word baptize or baptism only appears in the New Testament. John the Baptist began his ministry in AD 26 by preaching the necessity for repentance and the remission of sins. In as much as washing and cleansing were an important aspect of Judaism, it was accepted by many Jews as another rite of purification. The baptism of Jesus was not one of repentance or for remission of sin since Jesus had no sin to repent of, but it was the first act of his public ministry. Although there is no evidence that Christ baptized people, it is certain that He commissioned His apostles to do so in His name.

Following are short biographical sketches of the twelve disciples, in alphabetical order, and the apostle Paul:

- **Andrew**—He was born in Bethsaida and was a fisherman and follower of John the Baptist. He convinced his brother Peter to follow Christ. After preaching for a number of years following Christ's resurrection, Andrew was crucified at Patrae in Achaia, Greece, around AD 69. What was unique about Andrew's death is that he was crucified on a cross in the form of an X. To this day that type of cross is known as Saint Andrew's Cross.
- **Bartholomew**—He preached in India on the border of Persia, Armenia, Russia, and Turkey. Bartholomew suffered martyrdom by crucifixion in AD 58.
- **James, the son of Alphaeus**—He is also known as James the Less. His name only appears four times in the New Testament, each is in a list of the twelve disciples.
- **James, the son of Zebedee**—He was the elder son of Zebedee. James was a fishermen on the Sea of Galilee with his brother, John, and Peter and Andrew. James was one of the original twelve disciples and was the first martyred among the apostles. He was beheaded at the command of Herod Agrippa in AD 44.
- **John**—The brother of James the son of Zebedee, John was also a fisherman. Jesus loved John, and John sat at a place of distinction at the Last Supper. While hanging on the cross, Jesus committed the care of His mother to John. After Christ's resurrection, John began sharing the good news with others. He preached for sixty-eight years. John wrote the book of Revelation, which details the events that will surround the end of the world. He died a peaceful death because of old age on the island of Patmos, where he was banished.

Christianity and the Roman Catholic Church 49

- **Judas Iscariot**—He was chosen to serve as the treasurer of the group of disciples. Judas was the only one of the twelve who was not a Galilean. He betrayed Jesus to the Jewish authorities for thirty pieces of silver. Overcome with remorse after Jesus' arrest, Judas went back to the chief priests and elders and threw the money at their feet. He then went out and hanged himself. The priest took the "blood money" that Judas returned and bought a field that served as a burial place for strangers. This plot of land was called potter's field.
- **Matthew**—The son of Alphaeus, Matthew was also called Levi. He was a publican, a tax collector. When Jesus called him to follow Him, He changed his name to Matthew, which means "gift of Yahweh." Matthew was educated and was acquainted with Aramaic, Greek, and Latin languages. Matthew authored the first of the four Gospels of the New Testament probably in Antioch between AD 68–75. Matthew spent the first fifteen years in Judea and then the next twenty-three in Egypt and Ethiopia.
- **Peter**—Also known as Simon Peter, his date of birth is unknown but was probably around 20 BC, with his death occurring in AD 68. Jesus changed his name from Simon to Peter. The Greek translation of the Aramaic "Cephia" means "the rock." He was a leader and spokesperson for the apostles. The Catholic Church claims that Peter was the Bishop of Antioch, the ancient kingdom of Syria, from AD 33–40. The Catholic Church then states that Peter went to Babylon in Persia (now Iraq) from AD 40–44 before going to Rome to be the SEE, the official seat or center of authority of the Roman Catholic Church in AD 55. Peter was sentenced to death by Nero, and it is said that Peter requested to be crucified upside down because he did not feel himself worthy to be crucified like his Lord.
- **Philip**—A young, liberal Jew with some Greek influence, Philip was a close friend of John. Philip preached in Samaria in the center of Palestine in the territory now controlled by Jordan. He also preached in Hierapolis in Asia Minor, which is now Turkey. Philip preached against the worship of heathen gods, which incensed the pagan priests, who took him and bound him to a cross and stoned him to death.
- **Simon the Zealot**—Little is known about Simon the Zealot other

than the fact that he was differentiated from Simon Peter. The majority of scholars do not feel that Simon the Zealot is the same Simon mentioned as one of Jesus' brothers. It is believed that he traveled and preached with Thaddaeus, who was martyred at the same time as Simon the Zealot.

- **Thaddaeus**—He is also known as Jude. Most scholars feel that Jude, or Thaddaeus, is not the same Jude as Jesus' brother who wrote the book of Jude. It is believed that he preached in Judea, Samaria, Idumaea, Syria, Mesopotamia, and Libya. It is thought that he was killed with an ax in AD 65 in Beirut with Simon the Zealot.
- **Thomas**—A native of Galilee, Thomas was a fisherman by trade. He was of a doubting nature, and he did not believe in Jesus' resurrection until he saw Him with his own eyes and felt the scars in his hands. Nonetheless, he was heroic to the extent that he was ready to accompany Jesus to Judea and if necessary die with Him earlier in His ministry. Thomas spent years in India, Babylon, Syria, and Persia establishing churches and performing miracles. Thomas was mortally wounded by a lance thrust by a Hindu priest.
- **Paul**—He was born in Tarsus (Turkey) to a Pharisee, although he was a Roman citizen. He spoke Greek and Hebrew and was an educated man. His surname was Saul. As a Pharisee he agree to the stoning of Stephen, a church leader in the early church. Saul hated the early Christian church and did everything in his power to arrest the Christians. While traveling to Damascus to persecute a group of believers, a bright light blinded him on the trail, and he had a vision of the risen Lord calling him into service. He could not see for three days. A disciple by the name of Ananias taught him about the risen Savior before he departed from the city.

His life was in jeopardy in Damascus, so he escaped. The rest of his life he preached about Jesus to those who would listen. Paul met with the apostles Peter and James in Jerusalem for fifteen days where he learned more about Jesus and His time on this earth. Paul then continued preaching the good news to those who would listen.

Paul engaged in three mission journeys from AD 47–57. The first was with Barnabas, the second with Silas and Timothy, and the third by himself. After his mission journeys, he returned to Jerusalem where he was arrested. He was sent to Caesarea, a seaport in Palestine, under heavy guard. He was held in prison for two years. He appealed to Rome. His voyage to Rome is told vividly by Luke, who accompanied him on the trip.

In Rome Paul spent two years in a home with one guard. He was allowed visitor. Tradition tells of Paul's release, his visit to Spain, and his return to Rome as a prisoner once again. Paul died by the sword in Rome around AD 67, probably by Nero's command.

The Cross

The cross was a device used by many early nations of history for the execution of prisoners condemned to death.

The cross was a heavy stake set into the ground with a crossbeam set at right angles with the upright stake to extend above the crossbeam to accommodate the name of the one crucified and the crime for which he was executed. A projection from the upright stake upon which he could rest his feet to support his weight was seldom used.

The ancient Romans used the cross to fasten convicted persons to die. The cross is a symbol of the crucifixion of Jesus Christ and, hence, the Christian religion.

The cross before the Christian era was an instrument of a sentence of death, hence, the symbol implies suffering and loss. Among the Romans the practice of capital punishment by means of the cross continued until the fourth century when Constantine the Great abolished it.

There are various forms of a cross. Jesus died on the crux immissa, which is the Latin cross. With the triumph of Christianity, the cross became a symbol of great respect and reverence.

Crucifixion was a cruel method of execution whereby the condemned person was suspended upon a cross and allowed to die of exposure and exhaustion from intense suffering, lasting hours.

The Romans employed crucifixion as a means of executing outlaws and slaves in their provinces who renounced their masters, but Roman citizens were exempt from this form of punishment.

The apostle Paul was born a Jew, but by inheritance from his father, he was a Roman citizen. Condemned to death, he died by the sword in Rome about AD 67.

Crucifixion was used by the Romans in the persecution of the early Christians, but its use was finally abolished by Emperor Constantine. On the other hand, the Hebrews inflicted the death penalty by means of stoning, but under Roman domination they accepted crucifixion as a method of execution as well.

Specifically, crucifixion refers to the death of Jesus Christ upon the cross.

Resurrection

Resurrection is the reunion of the body and the soul after death. Life restored to the body once dead, is taught by Jesus, in his own words, and by the example of his own resurrection, John 5:28–29.

The Apostles witness the risen Christ and was one of the most essential aspects of their teachings. Apostle Paul taught that the body of man shall rise again, each one having its own identity preserved.

- 1 Cor. 15:20 But now is Christ risen from the dead, and become the firstfruits of them that slept.
- 1 Cor. 15:21 For since by man came death, by man came also the resurrection of the dead.
- 1 Cor. 15:22 For as in Adam all die, even so in Christ shall all be made alive.
- 1 Cor. 15:23 But every man in his own order; Christ the firstfruits afterward they that are Christ's at his coming.

First is defined as preceding all others, one thing after another in logical order, first also signifies others to follow.

In REV. 20:6 reference is made to a "First Resurrection," establishing at least by implication that there will be a "Second Resurrection" (Concordance).

Jesus promised his disciples he would return again one day to gather them unto Him.

- John 14:3 and if go and prepare a place for you, I will come again, and receive you unto myself, that where I am, there ye may be also.
- John 16:16 a little while, and ye shall not see me; and again, a little while and ye shall see me, because I go to the Father.

In faith, and the promise of Jesus this event has already occurred which was evidently after the death of the last Apostle the Lord Jesus returned to earth and brought forth the twelve, to abide with him in heaven.

This return of Jesus to earth, is not to be confused with the Lord's Second Coming.

Easter

The Christian Festival in celebration of the Resurrection of Jesus, held on the first Sunday after the date of the first full moon that occurs on or after March 21.

In older times the courts of Justice were closed and alms were dispensed to the poor, who were also fested in the churches. Slaves were sometimes given their freedom at Easter.

Many of the popular observances of Easter are pagan in origin. Some may be traced to the feast of the Goddess of Spring; "EOSTRA". The Easter Egg and Easter Rabbit are also pagan in origin.

Second Coming

In the Revelation of St. John, the Bible begins with the account of the Creation of the World and the first promise of a saviour who would redeem the world from sin. It ends with the promise of the Second Coming of Christ and the establishment on earth of the Kingdom of God.

The Second Coming of Jesus is in the Bible Scriptures and the Bible Concordance; Matthew 24:36, but of that day and hour knoweth no man, no not the angels of Heaven, but my Father only.

- John 5:28-29 marvel not at this; for the hour is coming, in which all that are in the grave shall hear his voice, and shall come forth; they that have done good, unto the resurrection of life; and they that have done evil, unto the resurrection of judgment.
- Matthew 24:31 and He shall send his Angels with a great sound of a trumpet and they shall gather his elect from the four winds, from one end of heaven to the other. (Elect – Chosen).
- Matthew 26:53 Thinkest thou that I cannot now pray to my Father, and He will at once give me more than twelve legions of Angels?

Legion is a chief unit of the Roman Army, composed in the New Testament times, of about 6,000 soldiers. The term came to signify a great multitude. Matthew 26:53. Host, the same as Legion, is used biblically for a multitude of angels.

- Matthew 25:32 and before him shall be gathered all nations; and He shall separate them one from another, as a shepherd divideth his sheep from the goats.

The Second Coming of Jesus to earth refers to Jesus return to rule for a 1,000 years, "Of that day and hour knoweth, no man,
- Matthew 24:36. There is no time, or event, in the Bible Scriptures, designating the time, or times, Jesus will visit the earth; "Christ the firstfruits, afterward they that are Christ at his coming.
- I Cor. 15:23. The same fact or event, stated above, of bringing forth other souls from the grave may have, (as distinguished from speculation or theory), may also have occurred.

Clergy—Ministers of Religion

The clergy are the body of ordained individuals who are responsible for the teaching of religious beliefs. In the Old Testament there is mention of Joshua serving as a minister or personal attendant to Moses. Also, ministers served at Solomon's court, and the Levites served as ministers in the tabernacle and temples.

Today, those who enter the ministry serve as leaders of Christian churches. They are entrusted with the responsibility of conducting worship services; administering the sacraments, the burial of the dead, and Parish duties; and managing the practical affairs of the church. The exact origin and very early history of the Christian ministry is uncertain.

The title rabbi came into use in the first Christian century as a title of respect by the Jews to teachers, masters, doctors, or the learned. Other titles of respect given to the clergy include reverend, pastor, father, and priest. The title rabbi was often applied to Jesus, and once to John the Baptist. The rabbi, usually the spiritual head of a congregation, is qualified to decide questions regarding the law and rituals. The rabbi is also given the authority to perform marriage ceremonies.

During the time prior to the Mosaic laws, individuals performed their own rights and determined what was wrong or right. Then Abraham and Isaac and Jacob established the patriarchal system, and those after them followed the appointed priests.

Christianity and the Roman Catholic Church

By New Testament times the teaching function of the priests had been taken over by the scribes who were known by the name of Pharisees. The Jewish priesthood came to an inglorious end with the destruction of Jerusalem by the Romans in AD 70.

In Palestine during this time the Pharisees, the interpreters of the Jewish written law and keepers of the oral law, emphasized the observance of the letter of the law but not the spirit of the Hebrew religious law. They pretended to be highly moral and virtuous without actually being so. The Pharisees had great political power. They were men with materialistic ambitions. People coveted the post of these high priests, who were like kings in their land.

The Roman Catholic priests are called father, a word with various scriptural meanings, including a begetter of children, that also refers to God's position (Eph. 4:6). The fathers of the church were the chief early Christian writers, whose works are the main source for the history, doctrines, and observances of the church in the early ages. The term church fathers also refers to those authors of the early Christian church who are recognized as high authorities in matters of church faith; in brief, the ancient classics of Christian theology.

The Roman Catholic Church sometimes regards Bernard of Clairveux, AD 1153, as the last of the fathers, while the Greek Church prolongs the age of the father until the Council of Florence in 1441.

Christmas

Christmas, originally named: "CRISTES MASSE"; The Mass or Church Festival of Christ. This is the English name for the season in which the birth of Christ is commemorated.

It is apparent, however, that a festival was celebrated at this season long before it was held sacred as the birthday of Jesus of Nazareth.

The Saturnalia, is the Roman festival of Saturn, and the winter festival of the heathen Britons. There is a summer solstice and a winter solstice; the time at which the sun reaches the farthest point North or South of the equator. Both were celebrated about December 25th; and later, the Roman festival in honor of the Sun-God; Mithra, about A.D. 273.

After its adoption by the Christian Church in the fourth century as the anniversary of Christ's birth , this name; "Christmas", was given a comparable interpretation.

The Christmas tree, a young Spruce or similar tree, with its branches gaily hung with ornaments and with gifts, is of Germanic origin. The tree, above all else is a thing of wonder, at Christmas time, Tannenbaum means Fir Tree.

Beginning in Rome about A.D.1038. Christmas began to be celebrated on 25 December of each year.

Early Church Leaders

The following Roman Catholic Church leaders impacted the church with their leadership and decisions.

Saint Basil (330–379) was an early church father who is recognized as the founder of Eastern Monasticism. He was also the champion of orthodoxy in the East. His doctrine favored the Trinity. Basil was an opponent of Arianism, which promotes that Jesus is not the same as God and that He was created by the Father. Roman Emperor Valens, an Arian, rigorously persecuted Orthodox Christians during his reign. Basil sought to promote unity between the two great branches of the church despite the fact that he refused to recognize the supreme authority of the papacy.

Theodosius I, the Great, (346–395) was a Roman Emperor who divided the empire into east and west. The Eastern Empire was known as the Byzantine Empire with its capital in Constantinople. The Byzantine Empire included Egypt, Thrace (Turkey), Moesia (Bulgaria), Macedonia (Yugoslavia), and Greece. The Western Empire was known as the Holy Roman Empire with its capital in Rome, including Italy, France, Spain, Britain, Ireland, Germany, North Africa, Sicily, and Sardinia.

Leo II (680–741) was called the Isaurian, Byzantine emperor, pope. His most famous act was the suppression of image worship, which had become prevalent in the empire, by an iconoclastic decree in 726. The decree specified that a graven image was of pagan or heathen origin and was forbidden on pain of death. This roused the fierce opposition of the bishops and monks. The bishops of the European provinces wanted images in the church. This brought about a separation of Italy from the Byzantine Empire in the church. In 733 Leo transferred Greece, Illyria, and Macedonia to the Patriarchate of Constantinople, capital of the Byzantine Empire of the East; thus initiating the separation between the Greek and Roman churches.

Leo III (742–816) served in the position of pope within the church. In 800 he invited Charlemagne, king of the Franks, to Italy, and on Christmas day he crowned him emperor of the Romans. This laid the foundation of the political system of the Middle East. Charlemagne opposed the decree of the Second Council of Nice in 787 in favor of images. Charlemagne was converted to Christianity by Bishop Wulfila, a Goth who had received an education in Constantinople to the Arian branch of Christianity.

Basil I (810–886) of Macedonian assumed the throne of the Byzantine Empire in 867. He sought to promote unity between the two great branches of the church despite the fact that he refused to recognize the supreme authority of the papacy. The controversy over images continued so long as the Asiatic provinces supplied the emperors their taxes and kept the peace.

The Roman Catholic Church

In general the pope is the supreme head of the church. The Roman Catholic Church claims that Simon Peter was the first pope, although there is not biblical evidence to support such a statement. The second pope was St. Linus (AD c. 67–c. 76). The Catholic Church acknowledges Jesus Christ as its invisible head and the bishop of Rome, otherwise known as the pope, as its visible head.

The bishops succeed in their function like the twelve apostles. The pope speaks with the assembly of his fellow bishops in what is known as a General Council. This excludes the possibility that error or novel doctrine will formally be taught in the church. Besides the Bible, tradition is the other source of teaching. At a later date the College of Cardinals, whose members rank next after the pope as church dignitaries, became more representative of the church throughout the world.

The official recognition of Christianity by the Roman Empire occurred in AD 313 when Constantine the Great was converted to Christianity by a vision that he had in 312. He moved the capital of the Roman Empire to Constantinople in 313, the city then called Byzantium. This made the pope virtually the ruler of Rome while still acknowledging the authority of the emperor. Sunday, the Lord's day, was first instituted as the Christian day of worship by Emperor Constantine in 321.

During the Middle Ages (476–1453), which marked the end of the Western Empire and the fall of the Eastern Empire, the temporal power of the church increased. Because of the increasing power of the papacy, the higher clergy became very influential. The close union between the church and the state culminated in the coronation of Charlemagne as the holy Roman emperor. During the Roman era, nations in a dispute would consult the pope and abide by his ruling on the matter.

The office of the pope is the final authority of the church, whether he speaks in concert with the assembly of bishops, the General Council, or alone.

The Council of Trent, which convened in 1545, reorganized the government of the papacy, redefined Catholic doctrines, and introduced reforms into the church, the religious orders, and the clergy. The reformation within the church was not based on the Trinity or Protestantism, but it did achieve permanent results within the church. It did not change the fundamental doctrines of the Roman Catholic Church. The supremacy of papal authority was finally maintained in July 1563 in the third session of the Council of Trent.

Following the Council of Trent, purification began in the church, and corrupt practices were eliminated. The Inquisition begun by Gregory IX to get rid of heresy within the church was reinstated to combat Protestantism in the form of a tribunal to investigate the practice of faith and morals of Christianity. Those found guilty of heresy and considered heretics were summoned before the Inquisition and given a trial and a sentence. At first the tribunal was lenient, but abuses soon crept in. Torture was adopted, property was confiscated, and burning at the stake was common. The papacy intervened but the abuses continued.

Heresy is the rejection of a belief that is a part of a church doctrine or opposed to official or established views of the church. A church member who holds beliefs opposed to church doctrine is determined to be a heretic.

In modern times there is a formal heresy, which is a deliberate denial of the truth revealed by the church, punishable by excommunication. Material heresy, which is the result of ignorance of the revealed truth, is considered blameless.

As long as a person believes in God, excommunication cannot be taken lightly. Excommunication did not entirely replace the Inquisition, only the punishment of a guilty sentence. Excommunication today is to be cut off from communion, sacraments, fellowship, and membership of the church.

The Protestant Episcopal Church

The Protestant Episcopal Church in the United States conforms to the practices and principles of the Church of England. The Church of England, while retaining its fundamental historic beliefs and ancient liturgy and practices, refused to give the pope any more authority than any other bishop. They recognized the Archbishop of Canterbury as the spiritual head of the church.

The Episcopal Church, as its name declares, is Protestant in nature. A spirit of liberalism has always been present in the church. So it has never committed itself to a doctrine of Scripture or to that literal interpretation of the Bible known as Fundamentalism. Herein is intellectual freedom.

Some religious scholars have held the view that the difference between Roman Catholicism and Protestantism is based on the fact that the latter recognized the absolute responsibility of the individual only to God, rather than to any church. During the Reformation, the name Protestant denoted no church. The reformers considered themselves evangelicals, thinking of themselves as reformers within, yet still a part of the Catholic Church.

The name Protestant was originally given to the followers of Martin Luther when they protested a decree of the Catholic Church passed in 1529 that stated that the Scriptures would only be interpreted by the church. Protestants recognized only the Bible as the source of supreme religious authority and the right of individual interpretation of the Scriptures, rather than to any church individual.

The Protestant Episcopal Church has no executor. The church government is one of democracy, whereas the people hold the ruling power or through elected representatives. Its presiding bishop holds no administrative power. No bishop has authority over any other bishop.

Having never committed itself to a doctrine of Scripture gives room for variation, for individuality, for independent thinking, and for religious liberty.

The Eastern Christian Church is the church of the countries comprised in the Eastern Roman Empire and the body of Christians owing allegiance to the Greek Church and observing the Greek rites rather than the Roman Church. The Greek Orthodox Christian Church of the Eastern Roman Empire, conforming to the Christian faith as represented in the beginning of the earliest time of the established doctrines.

The Western Christian Church is the Roman Catholic Churches of Western Europe and those churches elsewhere that are connected with or have sprung from them. The Western Christian Church is also that part of the Christian Church that acknowledged the pope after the split between Greek and Latin Christianity. The Latin Church is the Roman Catholic Church.

The Episcopal Church is governed by bishops and is the daughter of the Church of England, uniting it with all other Anglican churches who uphold the system or teachings of the Church of England.

A bishop in the Episcopal Church will ordain a candidate for the ministry who has passed the canonical requirements at the hands of the examining chaplains of his diocese. A clergyman so ordained may interpret Scripture, creeds, and church liturgy largely in accordance with his own conscientious beliefs so long as his faith is based on Scripture and is acceptable to the examining chaplains. These examiners themselves vary in their interpretation of the faith of the church. The Scripture and the creeds give room for variations for individuality, for independent thinking, and for religious liberty.

The *Book of Common Prayer* is the name given to the service book of the Anglican and Protestant Episcopal churches. The first book made obligatory to all churches in 1549 was revised in 1552. The church acknowledges two sacraments ordained by Christ as "generally necessary to salvation," namely, baptism and communion. No substantial alterations have been made in the Church of England's prayer book since 1662. The American version was compiled in 1783; the present American book was issues in 1928 after a period of fifteen years of revising.

Prominent Leaders

The Protestant Church had many prominent reformers who steadily moved from the Roman Catholic Church and eventually broke ties with Rome.

- **John Wycliffe** (1320–1384)—He was an English reformer who viewed the pope as the antichrist and the civil power over the church.
- **John Huss** (1369–1415)—He was a religious reformer who supported Wycliffe and his views and was condemned to death by the council as a heretic. Huss was burned at the stake.
- **Martin Luther** (1483–1546)—The great German leader of the Reformation who disagreed with the papacy and the church and broke

Christianity and the Roman Catholic Church

with Catholicism in 1517 after serving as a priest for ten years. Martin Luther was born in 1483 and was ordained to the priesthood in 1507. In 1517 Luther wrote to his bishop protesting the selling of indulgences. In defense of his position, Luther drafted *The Ninety-Five Theses*. Pope Leo X charged Luther with heresy because Luther stated that the papacy was not more divinely established than any other government, and he suggested his doubt as to whether the pope were the antichrist or his apostle. In 1525 he married Katharina von Bora, an adherent of the reformed faith that Luther was promoting. Luther's theological views eventually separated him from other reformers. In 1537 he formulated the Smalcald Articles for Protestant use. His last years were filled with sickness and depression. He died on February 18, 1546.

- **Ulrich Zwingil** (1484–1531)—A Swiss reformer who denied the right of the pope to decide questions in religion. In 1531 he was slain with other reformers in a dispute with Rome.
- **Philipp Melanchthon** (1497–1560)—A German scholar and theologian of the Reformation, he refused a divinity degree and became Martin Luther's assistant.
- **John Knox** (1505–1572)—A reformer and Scottish clergyman, he was a vocal opponent of the Catholic Church. He escaped assassination and died in Scotland.
- **John Calvin** (1509–1564)—A French reformer, he was a Roman Catholic before he turned to Protestantism. Calvin was friends with John Knox. He became a prominent writer for the Reformation. He was a pastor and professor of theology.
- **John Wesley** (1705–1791)—Wesley was founder of the Methodist Societies, which was originally within the Church of England but later separated. He traveled 5,000 miles a year on horseback preaching approximately fifteen sermons a week.

Jesuits

Jesuits are members of The Society of Jesus, a Roman Catholic religious order for men that was founded by Ignatius Loyola in 1534. The members take vows of poverty and chastity. A formula for the proposed new order was brought to Rome and presented to Pope Paul III in 1539. After a time the papacy approved and recognized the organization of the Jesuits.

The order expanded rapidly under the guidance of Ignatius, spreading into Spain, Germany, Italy, Portugal, Brazil, India, and Japan. In France the French Philosophic Party, a learned group of persons in the field of knowledge and principles, opposed the order on the grounds that it represented a powerful factor in the preservation of Catholic education and thought in the country. The intellectual training of the Jesuits is very thorough, necessitating years of study with emphasis being placed on the study of philosophy, theology, and humanities and science. There are four classes of Jesuits:

1. The novice engages in short periods of trial in spiritual exercises as prayer, reading, and meditation for two years. Then he takes the vows of chastity, obedience, and poverty.
2. He then becomes a scholastic. He studies, teaches, and undergoes additional spiritual training.
3. Next he becomes either a coadjutor, assistant priest, or an ordained priest. This requires that he meet the high standards required to become a professed father, which is the next step.
4. The professed father is required not only to reaffirm the three vows but also to take a special vow of obedience to the pope.

The order has a constitution and a father general. A general congregation composes the General Advisory Council and two representative deputies from each of the provinces, which are geographical divisions of the order.

The Jesuits founded schools and colleges in many of the principal cities of Europe, and for many years they were the dominant force in education on the continent. In the United States the Jesuits maintain many educational institutions, outstanding ones being Fordham and Georgetown universities.

In the various societies of Catholicism, the Jesuit order is strong and well respected around the world.

The Bible

Derived from the Greek phrase meaning, "the books," the Bible contains the sacred books of the Hebrew and Christian religions. Jews regard only the Old Testament as having religious authority. Christians revere both the Old and New Testaments.

Christianity and the Roman Catholic Church

Note: Literary texts were rare before 2000 BC, that is having to do with books and writings considered as having permanent value.

Discoveries of early manuscripts and their careful examination by scholars reveal clearly that the New Testament was for the most part written in the Greek of everyday speech. This provides justification for new and repeated translations into contemporary English, adjusting such translations to the latest discoveries of biblical research.

The Gutenberg Bible was the first printed version at Mainz, Germany, before 1456. Without a doubt, the Bible is the "best seller" and the most widely read of all books.

The King James authorized version dates from AD 1611.

In the Middle Ages there were many versions of parts of the Bible in vernaculars (belonging to or developed in a particular place, region, or country) and a few complete translations late in that period. The absence of printing and the small number who could read limited the demand and the use.

The knowledge of Jesus' words and deeds and the earliest phase of the Christian movement were themselves produced within that movement from 25 to 70 years after its beginning.

There is no reliable record of the making of the Old Testament Canon (any official recognized set of sacred books). The tradition that this was the work of Ezra (458 BC), or of a "great synagogue" in his time is pure legend.

The writings of the four Gospels were written approximately 40 years after the death of Jesus. Mark wrote his Gospel for Gentile Christians. Writings of the Gospel of Mark was followed by Matthew and Luke. The Gospel of Matthew was written mainly for Jewish Christians in Palestine about AD 70. The Gospel of Luke, himself a Gentile, wrote specifically for his Greek friend Theofhilus, but in general for the instruction of Gentile Christians. The fourth Gospel of John was not written by the apostle of that name, but by John who lived in Ephesus (colony of ancient Greece) near the end of the first century, his purpose in writing is not biographical or historical but evangelistic and is conjectural to some extent.

The books of Moses, Joshua, Judges, Ruth, Samuel, Kings, and many other writers of the Jewish prophets and teachers, including Amos, Isaiah, Micah, and Jeremiah.

The time between the Old and New Testaments was a period of about 400 years. The last historical chronicle of the Old Testament, the book of Nehemiah, a Hebrew leader who gained the favor of King Artaxeres Longimanus of Babylon (Iraq) and sent as governor of Jerusalem; Judea, c. 444 BC, carries the history of the Jewish people only up to the thirty-second year of the reign of Artaxeres (464–425 BC). This was about a century after King Cyrus permitted the Jews in 539 BC to return to their homeland from Babylonian captivity. Nehemiah in 433 BC found the Jewish people of Judea in the midst of Baal, a deity typifying the productive forces of nature and worshiped with much sensuality. Baal was a false god. Nehemiah, without delay, started a drastic reform.

The only account of the four centuries preceding the birth of Christ are from the Apocrypha, a group of fourteen books affirmed by the Catholic Church but denied by Protestant churches. Also are the questionable writings of Josephus (AD 37–100), a Jewish historian, public official, and general. His chief works, written in Greek, are *The Jewish War*, which gives a brief sketch of Jewish affairs from 170 BC to his day, and *Antiquities of the Jews*, which narrates the history of the Jews from Creation to AD 66. Josephus was granted freedom in AD 69 (he had been a prisoner of Rome after the Jewish War), and at that time he took the Roman emperor's family name of Flavius. He lived the rest of his life in Rome.

Chapter 5

Roman Rule to Muslim Domination

There was a gradual decline of the Roman Empire starting in AD 180 with almost continuous disaster. The Roman army was stretched to its breaking point with more mercenaries than Romans in order to control the occupied countries and to protect Roman roads and sea lanes. The army was also aggravated by constant plagues and famine.

Mohammed: Founder of the Religion of Islam

Mohammed was born in Mecca, Saudi Arabia, *c.* 570–632. At the age of forty, he received his first vision, which convinced him that he was called of God to establish a true religion—Islam. Based on the visions he received, Mohammed wrote the Koran, which Muslims believe to be the word of God, or Allah. The Koran instructs believers that only by submission to God can peace be achieved and that one should believe in Allah and the last days, angels, and the books of the prophets. Muslims believe in the prophets, such as Abraham, Moses, Jesus, and Mohammed. They believe that the angel Gabriel appeared to Mohammed and delivered messages to him as to what should be written in the Koran.

Mohammed taught a simple monotheistic religion that pointed to only one God, which stood in contrast to the previously prevalent Arabian polytheistic ideas of the worship of many gods. In the Muslim articles of faith, God is one person, there is no godhead. Also, in the articles of faith, it is stated that people are not born sinful. People are given free will and a mind to choose the right path or the wrong path, but they are first and foremost good.

The Koran adopts the mystical tradition or idea of seven heavens, which rise above one another like the stories of a building, with God residing in the seventh heaven. The Koran also states that there is life after death and that death is not the end of life but is the beginning of a better life.

In 622 Mohammed and his followers were pushed out of Mecca, but they waged a series of battles and in 630 Mecca surrendered. Mohammed died two years later, but Islam was well established and it spread to many countries throughout Europe, threatening Christianity. Because Mohammed left no heir or successor to carry on the work of Islam, a problem soon developed as to who should interpret the principles and laws of Islam. A division soon occurred, separating the Muslim world into Shiites and Sunnites.

The Shiites claimed Ali, Mohammed's cousin and son-in-law, as his successor. The Shiites rejected the "traditional law." They are essentially mystics whose morals are lax. Yemen, a country in southern Arabia, is predominantly Shiite. This branch of Islam has spread throughout Afghanistan and into India, but it has not moved west.

The Sunnites, or Sunnis, are a so-called Orthodox Muslim who approves the historical order of the first four caliphs as the rightful line of successors to Mohammed. They accept the Sunna, the traditional law based on Mohammed's writings and acts, as having authority concurrent with and supplementary to the Koran.

No matter the difference in theology, Muslims cannot be influenced by intoxicating drink, indecent clad women, or addictions to drugs, love, or money. Muslims fear God and no one else.

The Crusades: The Wars of the Cross

In 637 the Romans lost control of their empire in the east to Calif Omar and his Muslim followers. Then 400 years of Muslim rule followed. After a time, Muslim oppression of Christians led to the Crusades, the best known among them being the First Crusade from 1096–1099. In June 1099 the Muslims were routed from Antioch and the way to Jerusalem was opened. An army of 40,000 crusaders, the remnant of the vast army of 275,000, laid siege to Jerusalem. After five weeks the city was taken from the hands of the Muslims. The better part of Asia Minor was restored to the Greek Empire, and Edessa, Turkey, Antioch, Syria, Jerusalem, and Palestine were restored to the Latin kingdoms.

The Second Crusade took place from 1145–1149. In 1144 the country of Edessa was conquered by the prince of Mosul, Iraq, whose son advanced to destroy Jerusalem. St. Bernard of Clairvaux, France, foretold that the Second Crusade would end in disaster. The forces led by Conrad III of Germany were cut to pieces by the sultan of Iconium, Turkey, and the broken remnants were returned to Europe. But the death blow of the Latin kingdom came from Egypt; the Sultan Saladin invaded Palestine and disastrously routed the Christians.

The Third Crusade is perhaps the most famous. Its leaders were Philip II of France and Richard Lionheart of England. However, one by one the crusaders abandoned the cause, and in September 1192, Richard Lionheart made a truce with Saladin with the agreement that Christians would be allowed to pilgrimage to Jerusalem without interference.

There were a Fourth and Fifth Crusades of not much significance. The fourth never reached the Holy Land, and the fifth recovered by a truce with the sultan of Egypt, who maintained possession of Jerusalem and indeed a great part of the Holy Land.

The Sixth and Seventh Crusades began in 1244. In 1270 the last effort was made to take back the Holy Land from the Muslims; however, the effort failed.

The Knights Templar

The agreement that Richard Lionheart made with Saladin in 1192 remained in effect for a time thanks to the Knights Templar, a military order founded in early twelfth century to protect Christian pilgrims traveling to the Holy Land from attacks by Muslim zealots. The Knights Templar maintained forts in Acre, Antioch, and Tripoli, Libya. The order grew and became powerful and wealthy, because their forts served as safe storage for the gold, silver, and precious gems of the monarchs, of which the monarchs were charged a hefty price.

Enemies of the Knights Templar brought charges of corruption against the group. The impoverished king of France, Philip IV, cast greedy eyes on the treasures possessed by the Knights Templar, so he directed Pope Clement V to summon the Templar Grand Master to appear before him. The Grand Master, Jacques de Molay, and 140 knights appeared and were seized, imprisoned, and tortured. By 1314, with the execution of Molay and his knights, the order came to an end.

The Templar Knights patroled the Christian Pilgrims' route to the Holy Land of Jerusalem for over 200 years. Stories of their feats of courage can be found in many books, including the encyclopedia, under the heading, "Templars."

Islam Today

Muslim is the major religion across the Middle East and in Asia as is shown in the following table, which contains statistics from 2010.

Nation	Percentage of Population	Number of Muslims
Saudi Arabia	100%	26.5 million
Afghanistan	99%	28.2 million
Yemen	99%	20.5 million
Iran	98%	68 million
Iraq	97%	25.2 million
Palestine	95%	3.8 million
Egypt	94%	71 million
Indonesia	88%	213 million
Syria	88%	1.6 million
Lebanon	70%	2 million
India	15%	150 million
Israel	15%	1 million
China	2%	24 million

Chapter 6

Other World Religions

This chapter features information about various other world religions.

Buddhism

Buddha was born in *c.* 563 BC. His full name was Siddartha Gautama, and he was the son of an Indian Raja who ruled in northern India. At an early age Buddha's mind was occupied with the pain and grief of humanity's existence.

At the age of twenty-nine Buddha was married and had a son, but he was compelled to leave home and his family and search for wisdom. When he made this decision, he embarked on a life of contemplation and rigorous self-denial.

Once he was on the verge of utter collapse. Upon recovery he began to understand the utter folly of asceticism, the self-discipline of prayer and fasting and manual labor. He perceived that the only remedy for suffering as the result of existence was the extinction of selfish desires by focusing on tender emotions of love toward all people. With this new revelation he wandered from town to town sharing his new doctrine. As time went on he won more and more disciples, and an order was founded. He spread his teachings up and down the valley of the Ganges until his death in *c.* 483 BC.

His teachings center around self-sacrifice, contemplation, and suppression of all passions. Buddhism also teaches that each person must work out their own salvation through temperance, chastity, kindness, and brotherly love. Buddhists believe that the body and the senses can be brought under subjection until the being is absorbed in blissful nirvana, which is the extinction of life and the reunion with the eternal spirit of the universe. Buddhism recognizes no soul and, therefore, no future corporeal, having the nature of the body.

Buddhism is the world's fourth largest religion. Many people consider

Buddhism a philosophy and not a religion. Others refer to Buddhism as a cosmic religion, a complete, orderly, and harmonious religion that is free of dogmas and theology.

Tibetan Buddhists are the only sect who believe in reincarnation. The spiritual head of Buddhism in Tibet is the Dalai Lama, and up until Chinese took over the country, the Dalai Lama was the temporal ruler of Tibet, in addition to his service as spiritual ruler. Because of the belief in reincarnation, the Dalai Lama is supposedly the same person throughout all Tibetan history.

Buddha never wrote or documented anything. His students penned his words. It was at least 130 years after his death that Asoka, the emperor of India from c. 269–232 BC converted to Buddhism and made an attempt to write down the teachings of Buddha. Unfortunately, this caused dissent among the religion's followers and Buddhism faded in India and was replaced with Hinduism. Although Buddhism decreased in the country of its birth, it spread to surrounding countries in part because of missionaries who taught others its precepts. Buddhism was established in Nepal, Tibet, Burma, China, and Japan.

Hinduism

Hinduism is a religion and social system that is accepted and practiced by a majority of the people of India. This ancient religion believes in one god without denying the existence of others. Hinduism does not rest so much upon a basis of beliefs as it does upon a person's birth and their conduct.

Most of the religions of the world can trace their roots to a founder, but Hinduism is different in that regards. It makes no use of fixed creeds. It is very complex and variable.

The principles of reincarnation and Karma are widely accepted by Hindus. Life after death is a glorified continuation of the present existence. Hinduism is tolerant toward other religions, even assimilating parts of them.

The history of Hinduism started with the Vedic religion, the native religion of India, which was largely sacrificial, offering people and animals to various gods. With the deterioration of Vedic, Hinduism with its elaborate caste system became prevalent in about the fifth century BC. The Brahman are the highest members of the caste system, that of the priesthood. The lowest of the four Hindu castes is the Shudra. Penalties are inflicted for infractions of the rules of conduct. The doctrine of karma and transmigration of souls developed in the seventh century BC.

A variation of Hinduism came about in the sixth century BC called Jainism. This offshoot emphasized salvation by perfection and reverence for all living things.

Reformed Hinduism began with the invasion of Muslims in AD 1000. Further reform occurred as Western culture and Christianity entered India.

India and Religion

About 2000 BC a movement from the northeast brought a steady infiltration of Indo-European (Aryan) speaking people into the valley of the Ganges. It was formerly believed that the Aryan-speaking people were responsible for the introduction of civilization into India. It is certain that a lot of intermarriage between the Aryans of European stock and the aboriginal, native inhabitants of the land took place, absorbing into the social body under the name of Shudra, which later developed into the caste system.

In the Buddhist period, Asoka, emperor of India from 272–232 BC, was notable as a great monarch and a zealous propagandist of the doctrine and practice of Buddhism. His edicts prohibited the sacrifice of animals, medical relief for people and beasts, planting of trees, and sinking of wells. He preached the virtues of liberality, piety, and religious tolerance. History gives no details of this vanished system of principles or its fate in India.

The Mohammedan period was characterized by the invasion of India by the heartless army of Caliph Mohammed Tughlak in AD 1321. Tughlak's route of conquest pushed toward China, but it ended with a depleted treasury and an unpaid army of soldiers. Taxes to pay for his army were collected with fire and sword in the territory of Delhi in northern India. The spoils of war were usually sufficient to pay an army, but there was not much gold or silver in that part of India.

After Tughlak's rule ended in 1347, other Arab sultans ruled the territory of Delhi, ruthlessly putting to the sword all who dared to oppose them. Much later rebellions were suppressed partly by force of arms and partly by diplomatic relations.

The reign of the Arab sultans of India prevailed until 1631 when the British East India Company established factories in parts of India under a decree granted by the emperor of India. Gradually British occupation and expansion resulted in India becoming a British sovereignty.

Atheism

Atheism is the doctrine that there is no God. In the early times of the United States government, an atheist could not testify in an American court of law. In the eighteenth century the historical term atheist was applied to people who deny the existence of God, and the agnostic people who merely disclaim knowledge of God.

Theories of evolution in biology in the nineteenth century challenged older religious views of a special creation and the traditional interpretation of God, leading to a conflict between religious and scientific thought persisting in the present century. In theories of indeterminism and relativity, religion and science developed an area of mutual tolerance.

Chapter 7

Communication

In the eighth century BC the Aramaic language was marked off from its sister tongues. Through the Romans, Aramaic became the language of trade and diplomacy. Aramaic was the mother tongue of Jesus.

A notable change that took place in the conquered countries was the introduction of Latin. It was spoken in ancient Rome and was designated the official language by Julius Caesar in the second or first century BC. It was introduced for better communication and understanding and was to be adopted by all people of the annexed nations. The Roman Empire required that all peoples learn, understand, and speak Latin. This command was amazingly accomplished in a short period of time, in that all schools, colleges, etc., immediately held classes in Latin for students and community elders. Latin was certainly spoken in biblical times.

Aramaic is a Semitic language spoken in biblical times, including specifically the language used in Palestine after the captivity about 586 BC and spoken by Jesus and His disciples. Dating from about the tenth century BC, by Christian times it had become the speech of all Syria and Palestine, Mesopotamia (part of modern Iraq), Persia, and parts of Egypt. It was the mother tongue of Jesus and the original language in the books of Daniel and Ezra.

The language continued to be used after the disintegration of the Roman Empire in the fifth century; however, it progressively fell out of use as the popular tongue. In the end, the language was principally used by scholars, and it became the official language of the Catholic Church.

In 100 BC Latin attained its greatest prestige and widest distribution. In the growth and power of the Roman Empire the Latin language extended over the lands and people subject to the authority of Rome.

In addition to the Latin language, Latin literature dates back to 272 BC. When the Romans captured Tarentum, a Greek fortified seaport on the Mediterranean coast, and brought back Greek slaves to Italy, the slaves brought with them Latin literature, thus showing the depth of reach of the language. In early times, Latin literature consisted mainly of hymns, laws, and official records. Later, Latin was used in Greek dramas, both tragedy and comedy.

It is obvious that one must have a language in order to communicate, but how one communicates, sends and receives messages, is varied, and in ancient times, communication was done much differently than today.

In early times contending armies consisted of infantry and cavalry. The commanders often personally shouted their orders. Liaison depended on lung power to get the message across. Another form of communication was to send a courier, a messenger, who carried a verbal message to the recipient. Messages were also sent by carrier pigeons, smoke signals, flags, sun reflectors, horns, and bugles. Communication was obviously a challenge when trying to control a large army and effectively communicate battle plans.

Written messages obviously required a knowledge of a specific alphabet or language in order to transmit a message. Written messages were more practical since the message could not be misinterpreted, but the sender had to be educated, as did the receiver.

An example of an important piece of written information was a Letter of Marque giving permission for private citizens to capture enemies of the nation, specifically enemy merchant ships and cargo. These ships were commonly called privateers, which was the opposite of pirate ships that were not licensed or legal.

There are other forms of communication that some claim to possess that are mystical in nature. Some claim the powers of telepathy, supposed communication between minds by some means other than the normal sensory channels of speech and hearing. There are also the terms clairvoyance and clairaudience. Clairvoyance is the supposed ability to perceive things that are not in sight or cannot be seen. Clairaudience is the supposed ability to perceive and understand sound, often from a great distance, without actually hearing the sound.

In the distance mountain country of Tibet, located between India and China, the Buddhist monks who live in monasteries claim to have these types of communication abilities. Tibet, could be called, in a sense, a mystic or mystical country. They believe that one can achieve communication with God through contemplation and love without the medium of human reason.

The spiritual and temporal ruler of Tibet is the Dalai Lama. There are entertaining anecdotes and facts of history that still prevail of monks who, through sheer willpower and self-control, have obtained the power of telepathy and clairvoyance through years of priestly training.

Experiments carried out at a university claim to have proved the possibility of telepathy. However, most psychologists do not accept the theory that a response is possible without a stimulus operating through a known sense organ. Others have thought that it may be worthwhile to study this further.

Anecdotes collected and recorded over the ages have never been convincing to the scientific community. Anecdotes are subject to distortion by many retellings, as in the tales of telepathy from Tibet.

But beyond the anecdotes, Christians do not believe in supernatural communication or mystical powers. That work is of the devil, and it convinces many people to pursue higher communication with the spirit world.

Chapter 8

The Three Essentials Sustaining Humanity: Food, Clothing, Shelter

Ancient physicians and surgeons knew little about the human body. They knew the body was made up of different organs, but no universal names were applied to the organs until after the alphabetic system of writing was developed sometime during the Roman and Greek era.

One such system in the body is the digestive system. Just as it was from the beginning of time, food is made up of parts to form a whole in our daily lives. Not only is food essential for survival, but our lives revolve around how, when, and where we get our food to eat.

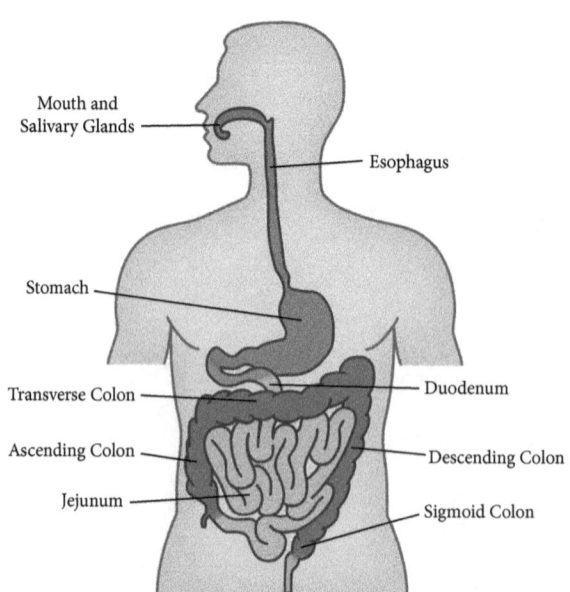

The Three Essentials Sustaining Humanity

The process by which food is converted into useful energy is called metabolism. It begins with a chemical process in the stomach and the intestinal tract that changes plant and animal food into less complex components like proteins, which is very important. This is not only because it is one of the three principle sources of energy but also because much of the body's structure is made up of proteins.

For example, the typical 160 pound male is composed of about 100 pounds of water, 29 pounds of protein, 25 pounds of fat, 5 pounds of minerals, 1 pound of carbohydrates, and less than 1 ounce of vitamins.

Because the muscles, heart, brain, lungs, and gastrointestinal organs are largely made up of protein, and because the protein in these organs is in constant need of replacement, getting enough protein in one's diet is important.

Carbohydrates are another essential energy source. They are also called starches or sugars. They are present in grains, fruits, and nuts. They are partly made up of proteins, but more often than not, they do not provide all the essential amino acids found in high protein foods. Carbohydrates are found in bread, cereals, flour, pasta, barley, legumes, and rice.

Simple carbohydrates on the other hand are pure sources of calories and contain little nutritional food value. They are found in such foods as table sugar, candy, pastries, and soft drinks. It is for this reason that they are often termed "empty calories."

Fat is another essential energy source and is of various solid or semisolid oily or greasy materials found in animal tissue and in the seeds of plants composed of glycerides, an odorless, colorless, syrupy substance that can be liquefied. They appear in the form of butter, salad oil, and fats in meat.

Fats are also classified as saturated or unsaturated. The saturated type of fat tends to be solid at room temperature. In general, fats in foods of plant origin are more unsaturated than in those of animal origin, except for coconut and palm oils, which are highly saturated.

Fats play several essential roles in the metabolic process. First, they provide more than twice the number of calories on a comparative weight basis than do proteins and carbohydrates. (One gram of fat contains nine calories.) They also can be stored in the body in large quantities and used as a later energy source.

Amino acids contain various elements, including nitrogen, which is a colorless, tasteless, odorless chemical element forming nearly four-fifths of the atmosphere. It is a component of all living things and used by plants and animals in the formation of proteins.

There are twenty-two different amino acids that are essential for the body's protein needs. Nine of these must be provided in the diet; these are thus called essential amino acids. The rest can be synthesized, compounded by elements in the body itself.

Vitamins, which are present in foods in their natural state, are necessary for normal metabolism and for the development and maintenance of the structure and function of various tissues in the body. The recommended daily allowance is generally expressed as RDA.

The vitamins are A, B, C, D, E, K, and P. Vitamins are any number of unrelated, complex organic substances found variously in most foods or sometimes synthesized by forming elements together in the body.

Minerals are another component of the basic nutritional needs. All living things extract them from the soil, which is their ultimate source. Like vitamins they are needed for normal metabolism and must be present in the diet in sufficient amounts for the maintenance of good health. The essential minerals include calcium, phosphorus, magnesium, iodine, iron, zinc, selenium, copper, manganese, fluoride, molybdenum, and chromium. Vitamins and minerals are essential for the regulation of metabolism and normal growth and functioning of the body.

Medicine—The Science of Healing

The actual records of medicine begin with the dim and vague Babylonian, Egyptian, and Greek cultures. Surgery in Egypt was preformed as early as 2200 BC as depicted on the tombs of the Pharaohs. The medical ideas of the Egyptians and the Babylonians were carried westward to Greece and Rome.

The birth of medical science began with Hippocrates in 460–377 BC and then Aristotle, 384–322 BC. Roman medicine was largely in the hands of Greek physicians. Celsus, AD 14–37, wrote a book about Roman medicine that was widely used. About 100 years later a controversial name in medical history came on the scene. Galen (AD *c.* 129–199) practiced in Rome and developed an elaborate system of medicinal herbs that were used in place of drugs. The writings of Hippocrates and Galen dominated medical thinking well into the sixteenth century.

"A wealthy property owner always fed his Guards, Servants, and Slaves, healthy foods, as sick workers were costly and of no benefit to him.

In the gardens on the property were always seven (7) vegetables, 2 of which were always Garlick and Onion, which were known to have Medicinal Properties for curing, healing, or relieving."

Galenus, Claudius (Galen). A.D. 131–c200

A Greek physician who was appointed surgeon to the Gladiators in A.D. 157. He gained renown for his methods of diagnosis and prognosis.

For some 14 centuries Galen's 100 Extant Treaties; still existing, not extinct, were regarded as authoritative by the medical profession. As an Anatomist Galen's errors were many and great, because he based his conclusions on what he had observed in dissecting Apes, swine, and other lower mammals.

Vesalius, Andreas 1514–1564

Was born in Brussels, Belgium. Studied at the Universities of Louvain, Belgium, and Paris, France.

After serving as a Military Surgeon in the Imperial Army he became professor of Surgery and Anatomy; the dissecting of an animal or plant in order to determine the position, structure, etc. of its parts at the university of Padua, city in N. Italy.

As a result of his dissections on the bodies of hanged criminals he came to realize that much of the Anatomical knowledge handed down from the time of Galen was untrustworthy. This was largely because that ancient physician's works dealt with the anatomy of monkeys, dogs, and other lower animals.

In 1543 he published "De Humani Corporis Fabrica Libri Septem" which was the first exact and complete treatise on Human Anatomy based on actual observation. The book was admirably illustrated with more than 300 woodcuts by Johann Stephan Von Kalkar, a pupil of Titian, a renown Italian painter.

After leaving the University in 1544 he became physician in-ordinary first to Charles V, then to his son Philip II.

Dentistry and Barbering

The science of dealing with the treatment of oral disease is known as dentistry. This includes hygiene, cleaning, extraction, and later fillings, crowns, and the construction of artificial dentures. Early dental treatment began in Egypt and other Eastern civilizations, but it was extremely crude. In Europe in the nineteenth century, barbers were the official teeth pullers.

Reference is made to the barber's razor in the Old Testament (Ezek. 5:1), and barbers were known in Greece and Rome.

The sign of the barber (a pole with spiral bands of red and white) symbolizes the old function of the barber: bloodletting, i.e., the opening of a vein to remove blood. Blood is the fluid, usually red, circulating through the heart, arteries, and veins.

The leech is any of a number of mostly flattened worms living in water or wet earth and having a well-developed sucker at each end. Most are bloodsuckers and one species has been used in medicine. In former times the leech was used for bloodletting of patients. On research, no definite purpose for bloodletting could be found.

Although barbers shave and trim beards and cut hair, many barbers were surgeons and dentists. Their surgeon duties pretty much consisted of bloodletting. Some believe that barbers were given this role because their barber chair could be adjusted to lean or lie back, thus giving them easy access to treating someone's mouth.

Two important contributions to dentistry were the introduction of anesthesia and the X-ray machine. X-rays were discovered in 1895 and were soon used in dental surgery. General anesthesia, cocaine in 1858 and Novocain in 1904, helped the patient to be more comfortable during dental procedures.

Food Preservation

Food is commonly understood to include animals and vegetables. In the early history of the world, all food that was consumed was eaten raw, and it came from animal and vegetable sources that already existed. Later people learned to alter the taste and appearance of the natural foods by cooking them. Still later, both animal and vegetables was raised and cultivated for food.

Preservation is the protection of food against spoilage. After foods have been picked or harvested, colors begin to fade, the texture changes, and flavors gradually disappear. Freezing is the most effective method of food preservation. Historically, it is believed that even cave dwellers knew that meats left packed in ice or snow remained edible for long periods of time. The early

Greeks and Romans packed food in snow brought from the mountains by laborious relay systems.

Safeguarding health by ensuring the purity and safety of foods goes back to the dawn of civilization. The book of Leviticus in the Old Testament contains specific food laws.

Another form of preservation was to use salt and a drying technique. Food dehydration is used to preserve foods through the removal of water like sun drying of grains—corn, wheat, rice, and rye—and grapes, which become raisins.

To sustain people groups, travelers, large armies, and the crew and passengers of large ships, the bulk of their food came from dehydration of grains.

Animals

Goats and sheep date back to ancient times in both wild and domesticated form. These animals are both cud chewing mammals and are common throughout the world. They are bovine animals considered in manner as slow witted, meek, timid, or oxlike. The bovine family consists of cattle, buffalo, deer, goats, and antelope.

Goats are restless, inquisitive animals. Their food consists mainly of grass and leaves and shoots of bushes and trees. They are of the bovine family and closely related to sheep. Despite its name and appearance to goats, the Rocky Mountain goat of North America is not a true goat. It is classified as a goat-antelope.

Sheep are ruminants. They were among the first animals to be domesticated, for they could furnish people's basic needs. They provided heavy wool for clothing, flesh for food, and skin for making leather footwear or other products.

Goats were extensively raised in Palestine for food, milk, wool, and their hides. It is a clean animal, but they are quite destructive. They gnaw at things and use their horns to peel off bark from shrubbery and trees. Much of the barrenness of Palestine has been attributed to goats.

In the Bible there are many mentions of sheep and goats. Jesus even uses the two animals to signify the righteous and wicked people at the end of time.

Another information animal in ancient times was the horse. The earliest evidence of the origin of the horse dates back to the plains of Mongolia some 3,500 years ago. Domesticated for drawing wagons or carrying heavy loads and riders, the horse was, and is, an important farm animal.

Pigs are domesticated animals with a long, broad snout and a thick, fat body covered with coarse bristles. Meat from a pig is called pork. All domesticated pigs are probably descended from the European wild boar. Their recorded history dates to the sixteenth century at which time two distinct types had emerged, one for bacon and the other for lard and ham. These two basic types are readily recognized by pork producers.

Of the seven popular breeds in the United States, the Poland China was developed in Ohio and rates as the largest pig. The boars grow to weigh about 1,000 pounds, and the sows can weigh up to 800 pounds.

Writings in the Bible refer to pigs and hogs as swine. They are always referred to as unclean animals, notably in the parable of the prodigal son.

In the Bible the horse is nearly always mentioned in connection with warfare. Nowhere is it referred to as a beast of burden. War horses were common in Egypt and Assyria, an ancient and powerful empire located along the Tigris River. The Assyrians are mentioned in the Bible mainly for their warlike aggressions in the later half of the eighth century BC.

The Israelites used horses because of the ruggedness of the terrain which made chariot warfare difficult. It was significant that Jesus did not ride a horse on His triumphal entry into Jerusalem. Instead, Jesus rode on a beast or burden, an ass, otherwise known as a donkey or burro. Resembling a horse, a donkey has longer ears and a shorter mane than the horse. Domesticated and serving as slow, patient, sure-footed animals, they complemented the work of the mule, ox, or camel in Palestine.

The Three Essentials Sustaining Humanity

Hunting

Hunting game and wild birds for food has been going on since the early days of history. Ancient Assyrian and Egyptian drawings depict hunters pursuing wild beasts. Hounds were often used to track game. The Greeks hunted big game on horseback or by trapping.

Big game included all wild mammals larger than the ordinary fox, such as deer, elk, bears, wolves, wild boar, wild sheep, etc. Small game included rabbits, raccoons, opossums, squirrels, ducks, quail, partridge, pheasants, geese, doves, pigeons, etc.

Main Food Source

Today the staples of the world are rice and wheat. Rice is a humble and modest food. A cereal grass of Asia, rice is the staple food of more than half the inhabitants of the world. Some believe that it was first harvested in China more than 5,000 years ago. Rice was introduced into Italy around 1470 AD, into South America is 1530, and into the Virginia colony in 1647.

A nutritious and easily digested food that is in constant demand and in commerce, it is an important commodity in world trade.

There is no reference of rice in the Bible; however, wheat is mentioned in both the Old and New Testaments. Wheat is the major food crop of the temperate regions of the world where it is not too hot or cold. Wheat is second only to rice as a worldwide means of sustenance.

Egypt cultivated wheat from the early development of the country. Egypt was the granary of the Mediterranean with much of the wheat going to Rome in that early period of history.

Bread

In ancient times, people baked bread on hot smooth stones. The first breads were probably made of coarse meal of acorns, beechnuts, or other wild grains mixed with water and baked at first in the sun and later on the fire. The first known breads were flat, hard, and rough in structure. Because of crude milling methods, the grains were insufficiently ground and were visible in the bread.

To make bread, cleaned and sifted grains were first reduced to flour by pounding or grinding. The flour was then mixed with the liquid and kneaded before baking.

In early times bread was made chiefly of barley or wheat, but other ingredients might be added. Loaves were circular in shape and about an inch thick.

The Romans had more than seventy kinds of bread, ranging from the "Senator's" bread, which was white and fine, to the course black bread of the peasant.

The Romans used a leaven process to make bread rise. A small piece of fermenting dough was put aside to be used in a fresh batch of dough to make it rise before or during baking. Large scale bread backing is humanity's earliest attempt.

The universal food of mankind, Bread is man's oldest manufactured food.

Some forms of bread must have been made before the dawn of history, fossilized remnants of it have been found: 10,000 years ago in Swiss Lake Dwellers habitats.

Probably the first breads were made from the coarse meal of acorns, beechnuts, or wild grains, mixed with water and baked at first on flat stones heated in the sun, later by fire.

Bread is mentioned in the Bible and was of such importance in biblical times that the word itself was synonymous with food in general.

The first breads baked, over hundreds of years were unleaven bread; flat, thin; a mixture of milled ground grains and water.

Then it was discovered that by taking a piece of dough, laying it aside to ferment, then inserting, a small piece of it into a fresh batch of dough caused it to rise, thus a leaven bread made by a fermenting Sour Dough.

Yeast

Any of various single celled fungi is the yellowish, moist mildews mass of yeast plants occurring as a froth on fermenting solutions. This substance dried in flakes or granules or compressed into cakes for preservation.

Yeast, previously was used in making beer and whiskey, and now as a leavening in baking.

Sour Dough Bread, baked by using fermenting dough, has always been baked and is preferred by many people over full grain bread.

Fire

From the earliest ages, fire has been a source of heat and a primary method for cooking food. The difficulty of starting the flame was so great and the desire of never allowing it to be extinguished gave rise to the maintaining of fires.

Early methods of producing fire were the rubbing together of two pieces of wood or the striking of flint and steel together to produce a spark. One of the simplest methods is what is called the fire plough in which a pointed stick runs along a grove in a piece of wood lying on the ground. Other methods include the bow drill of the Eskimo and the pump and drill of the Iroquois Indians.

Human culture may be said to have begun with fire, of which the uses increased in the same ratio as culture itself.

Clothing

Wearing apparel is essential for human welfare. The progress and growth of the clothing industry has been enormous with the growth in population of the earth. Clothing from ancient times to present was manufactured or made from fur, cotton, silk, or leather.

Wool

Wool is the fleecy hair of sheep and a few other animals such as the llama, angora goat, cashmere goat, which is raised chiefly in Tibet, and the camel. This type of apparel has been known and used since prehistoric times and has long been one of the most important fibers used by humans. Wool is classified under three general headings: (1) carding or clothing wools, (2) combing or worsted wools, and (3) miscellaneous or carpet and blanket wools. This classification is based on the length, fineness, and felting qualities of the staple.

Through many centuries of breeding, selection, feed, protection, and careful handling of the wool-bearing animals, the wool has been developed by continuing improvement in the fineness of the wool, its length of staple, and its adaptability to various used.

Leather

Leather is the hide or skin of animals that has been dried and subjected to certain chemical processes known as tanning, in order that decomposition may be arrested.

In history it is certain that the ancient Hebrews knew the principle of tanning leather with the use of oak bark, which they may possibly have learned during the captivity in Persia.

Leather sandals and other articles made from animal hides that show the effect of the thorough curing and tanning have been found in Egyptian tombs known to be more than 3,000 years old.

The Greeks used leather early in their history. The Orientals, according to existing records, knew how to make leather before they formed systems of writing. Both in the New and Old Worlds, leather and furs were the first clothing used in colder climates.

Leather was also an important addition to a warrior. It was their only armor prior to the use of metals. The earliest coats of chain mail ever used were leather. The Anglo-Saxons made all their armor of leather.

The types of leather are the hides and skins of different animals and are suited for many different uses. They are now used in the many industries that convert leather for varied products. The many types of hides and skins are cow and bull hides; steer hides; calfskins, kid, and goatskins; sheepskins, kangaroo, and wallaby skins; pigskins, ostrich, snake, lizard, shark, walrus, and seal skins; horsehides; buffalo hides; alligator and crocodile skins; as well as the skins of other reptiles and the hides and skins of sub-branches of animal families.

Technological progress in the science of tanning has made tremendous strides in the past century.

Cotton

Cotton has been cultivated for more than 3,000 years. The soft, white seed hairs filling the seed pods of the cotton plant can be made into thread and woven into cloth.

Cotton was raised in India as early as 1800 BC. The Mohammedans introduced the crop into Europe. Columbus found it already in cultivation when he reached the West Indies. The wide distribution of cotton in early times indicates that the crop may have arisen independently in more than one area.

For best growth, cotton requires a hot, humid climate and a long growing season free of frost for at least 200 days.

Cotton is picked between September and December. Dry weather is necessary for this operation because moisture will injure the quality of the fibers.

Once it is picked cotton is ginned, which separates the fiber from the seed, then it is baled and shipped to market for purchase by a manufacturer.

Cotton once supplied nearly nine-tenths of the raw material going into clothing for the countries of the world. Cotton has been replaced in many cases by various synthetic fabrics that, since World War II, have been produced in greatly increasing quantities. Cotton nevertheless continues to play an important role in the world's economy, and it still ranks first among the fiber crops of the world.

Silk

Silk is the fiber produced by the silkworm to form its cocoon. The fiber is exceedingly fine and strong.

The history of silk textiles dates from about 2600 BC, where China produced the first silk garments. Some 2,000 years later the Chinese gave silk to the Persians, and they in turn carried it to the Western nations.

In the first and second centuries BC, the Greek and Roman aristocracy used silken garments, but all raw silk was imported from China. Until AD 555 the secret of production was stolen from China by the direction of the Roman Emperor Justinian.

This was the beginning in Europe of an industry that soon spread rapidly, reaching the Western nations by the sixteenth century.

Chapter 9

Minerals and Tools

A mineral is a metal occurring in nature that can be obtained by mining. Minerals and metals have played an important role in history as a form of payment and as a building material.

Minerals

Gold is a precious yellow metal that has been prized from the earliest of times. Gold was one of the first metals used by humans. Archeologists have discovered gold fishhooks made by primitive human beings. Cups and jewelry made from gold and estimated to be from as early as 3,500 B.C., were found in what is now known as Iraq when excavating, looking for evidence of the biblical flood. Gold is highly malleable and free of the liability of corrosion. Coins made of gold, of a specified weight and fineness, represented set values and were used for bartering as early as 1800 BC.

Gold was associated with the Golden Age in Greek and Roman mythology to represent the best age of the world when humanity lived in innocence and happiness.

Silver is another fine mineral, but it is second to gold. A white, malleable, metallic element, silver was also used in the making of coins. Silver, too, had a specified weight and fineness as a unit of monetary value.

The Monetary Value of Gold and Silver

A Talent is any of various large units of weight or of money, varying with the time and place.

Attica, a city in ancient Greece (Athens), placed the value of the Talent, which is the weight of gold and silver as a monetary unit, this value was recognized and used in Greece, Rome, the Middle East, etc. The term "Talent" as a monetary unit is mentioned in the Bible Scriptures during Jesus' time.

The Attica Talent is estimated to have weighed about 58 pounds. This weight, in the English and American system of weights is called Avoirdupois, and is based on a pound of 16 ounces.

The value of the Hebrew Talent of gold at that time, being estimated at about $30,000.00; and that of the Hebrew silver unit at about $2,000.00. Whereas, the Attica silver unit at about $1,000.00 - $1,200.00.

Gold in Troy weight: 12 ounces = 1 Pound

Gold in Monetary weight: 16 ounces = 1 Pound

Copper is a malleable metallic element that has a reddish-brown color. Metals like bronze are composed of copper and tin. Brass is made up of copper, zinc, and nickel. To make silver and gold coins harder, it was discovered that a small amount of copper can be mixed with the silver or gold.

When minerals were discovered they were often shaped into tools and implements, but stones were still used quite often as tools. The Stone Age marked a time in history where stone implements were constructed and used extensively by human beings.

Bronze is a durable, metallic brown alloy consisting essentially of copper and tin. It was probably discovered by accident, but the mixing of copper and tin resulted in a stronger metal that became a favorite material of Greeks and Romans for their many public monuments and statues because it held up well to the elements. Most of these monuments have been lost because of the value of the metal and the ease which it could be recast. The Bronze Age signified the discovery of this metal and its use.

Iron is a malleable, silver-white metallic element that is scarcely known in its pure form, but is abundantly used in its crude or impure forms. The Iron Age of history was marked by the use of iron implements. This age followed the Stone Age and Bronze Age.

Weighing Machines

The platform scale is a raised horizontal surface of wood or metal that was invented by Thaddeus Fairbanks in 1830 and had its origin in the balance, which was first used by the Egyptians in 2500 BC.

The scale balance is an instrument for comparing the weight of two objects. A scale often features two shallow pans hanging from either end of a lever

supported exactly in the middle by a stand. With a scale, one pan is for a set weight while the other is for the object to be weighed. The scale pans should be in equilibrium, a state of balance or equality between opposing forces when the scale pans are empty.

On the other hand, a bar lever is a device consisting of a bar turning about a fixed point, using power or force applied at a second point to lift or sustain a weight at a third point. A bar is any piece of wood, metal, etc., that is longer than it is wide or thick, often used as a lever.

The spring balance has a cylindrical coil of spring wire in a vertical case that is more complex than the lever. Although the spring balance is inherently less accurate, it is far more rapid and convenient to use.

Until approximately 1917 scales were used mainly for determining weight in commercial trading. Since then many specialized weighing machines have been developed, especially in the area of electronics.

Ancient Measurements

An ancient measurement was the cubit, which was the length of the arm, from the tip of the middle finger to the elbow. A cubit was approximately eighteen inches in length. Noah's ark was measured in cubits. The completed vessel measured 300 cubits in length, 50 in breadth, and 30 in height (it had three stories).

Minerals and Tools 91

Engraving from Mechanics Magazine—Circa 1824

Chapter 10

The Human Race and Human Body

The human race is made up of various groups of persons connected by common descent, blood, or heredity. The question may be asked, "Are all people created equal?" The *New World Dictionary* defines equal as having "the same quantity, size, number, value, degree, intensity, quality, etc.; having the same rights, privileges, ability, rank, etc.; evenly proportioned, having the necessary ability, strength, power, capacity, or courage to challenge; and any thing or person that is equal to be the equal of another and to make uniform."

The problem of how the races of humanity were originally differentiated is a most difficult one to which only hypothetical answers can be given. Race as a scientific concept has to do only with physical form. All existing human beings are of one species, Homo sapiens, and are thus very much alike.

A human being is a primate, which is any order of mammal, including humans, that is characterized by flexible hands, feet, and forward-facing eyes. Within the Homo sapiens genius there are different races: Negroid, mainly from eastern and southern Africa; Caucasoid, mainly from Europe, northern India, the near East, and northern Africa; Mongoloid, mainly from Asia, China, and Korea. There are obviously mixtures of these races as people have married between races throughout history.

The Human Race and Human Body   93

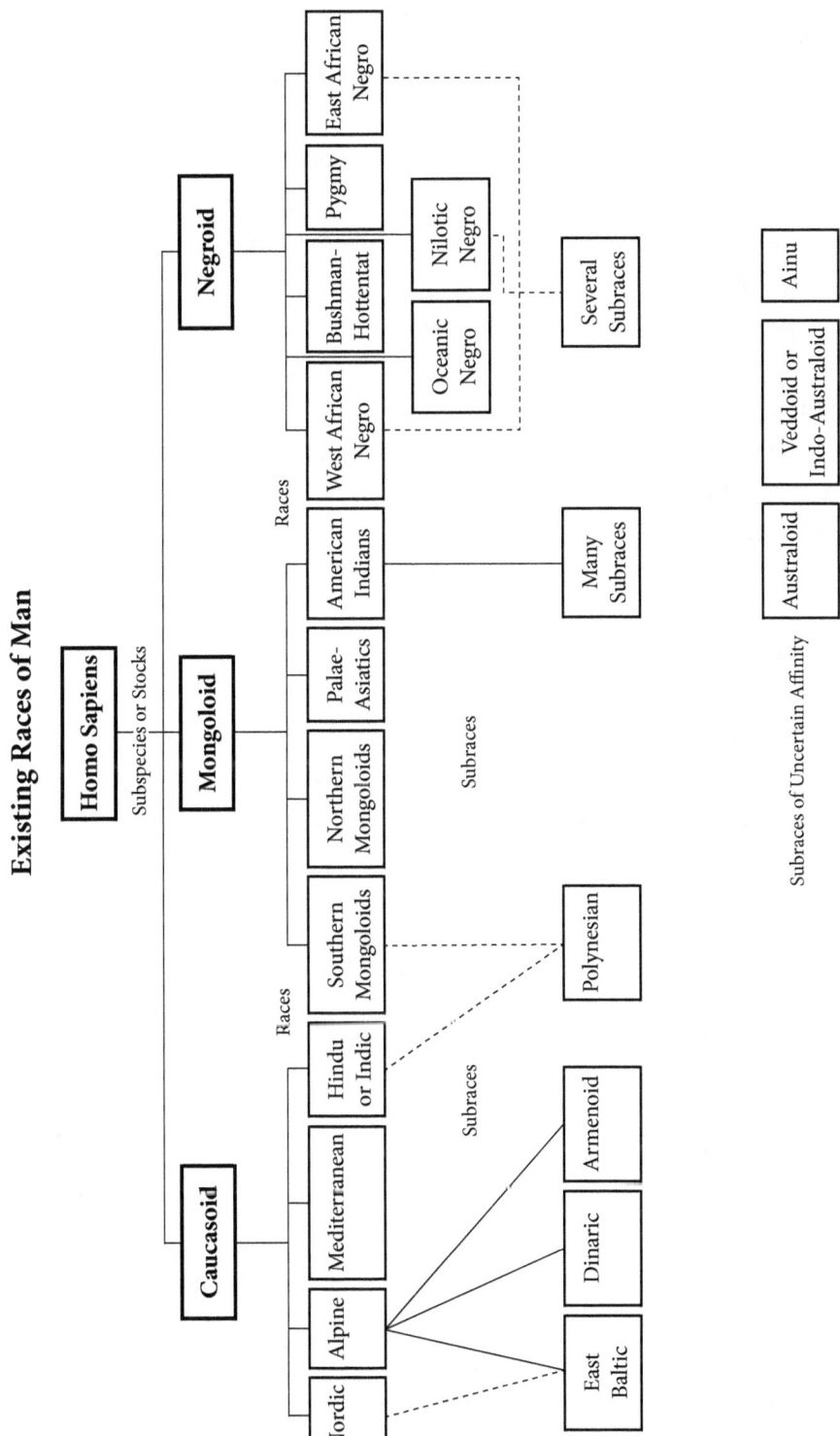

Race

The human race refers only to large groupings of mankind, the members of which resemble each other closely in physical characteristics but who differ from other human beings by being closely related through heredity.

Also any of the different varieties of mankind,- distinguished by form of hair, color of skin and eyes. Race is a population of people that differs from others in the relative frequency of some Gene or Genes.

The three main Division of Mankind are Caucasoid, (White); Mongoloid, (Yellow); Negroid, (Black); based on physical characteristics, belonging to most of the races and subraces of the world.

All existing human beings are of one species; Homo Sapiens, and hence are much: alike. Some traits such as head forms, character of hair, facial protrusion and etc.

Taste is one of the five senses of man, and is capable of distinguishing between sweet, sour, salt, and bitter.

Taste is a style reflecting such preferences on the part of a group of people of a particular time and place. Sense of taste is primary, in the taste of ones intellectual liking.

Sense of taste begins with the palate in the roof of the mouth and is in conjunction with the taste buds on the surface of the tongue.

This divides mankind into three subspecies; Caucasian, Mongoloid, Negroid. Note, consult Anthropology, for a detailed history of the three races.

Caucasian

The Caucasian, same as (Caucasoid), people, so named because the native people of "Caucasus", a mountain range considered to be the boundary line between Europe and Asia Minor, and lying between the Black Sea and the Caspian Sea are generally considered as a type symbol, showing the characteristics of a group as to be a representative example of the Caucasian group of people.

The Caucasian people is a designation of one of the major groups of mankind, it includes peoples of Europe, North Africa, the Near East, India, etc., and is loosely called the White Race, although it embraces many peoples of dark skin color.

The principal group of Caucasian are located in Europe. The Caucasian are in general, tall with high arched foreheads, long, narrow noses, thin lips, and strongly developed chins. They usually possess long, narrow, high heads and moderately narrow faces.

Mongolia

The Mongoloid group of mankind, (The Yellow Race), located on an extensive tableland lying partly within China and partly outside its northern border of the Soviet Union.

The region it designates also includes, geographically, Tannu-Tuva, a region in Russia in the west and a section of Manchuria in the east.

Mongolian history begins in the 12th century. Genghis Khan (1162–1227) consolidated the Mongolian plateau and created a man power reserve for his invading armies. Genghis, and to some extent his heirs, wanted to acquire by loot and by loot alone, the goods produced in the permanent cities of the vanquished.

Genghis Khan in order to acquire more producing profitable land, proceeded south into China. He captured Peking in 1215, razing towns, burning fields, and slaughtering peasants. The conquered land was turned into an extension of Mongolia.

About 1644 the Mongols overthrew the Sung Dynasty and proceeded south through China as far as North Korea. South Korea had adopted a policy forbidding their lands to Chinese Colonists.

Genghis Khan's grandson; Kublai Khan, 1216c–1294; his successor established a great Mongolian Empire and was Emperor of China 1260c–1294, with China as only a part.

But the Mongols soon after became quarrelsome among themselves with a falling out and degenerated after Kublai Khan's death.

Chu Yuanchang, founder of the Ming Dynasty (1368–1644), raised a patriotic force and drove the Mongols back to their desert.

The Japanese people are a composite with some distinct characteristics of the Mongolians, but with the skin type of the Polynesians, not the Mongol, (Yellow Race).

The Polynesians are brown-skinned, short in stature, black haired people which includes Hawaii, Samoa, etc., and the Malayan Archipelago.

Negroid

Negroid is a term with three sets of meanings according to its use as a racial, ethnic, or social-class term. Racially, it designates a major subvariety of the human species whose distinguishing physical characteristics include dark skin color ranging from various shades of brown to black, crinkly or woolly hair, longish heads, broad nose structure, pronounced jaw and lips, and generally tall in stature.

The Negro race, in common with all other racial varieties has moreover its relatively lighter black and relatively darker or brownish type hair.

Negro as an ethnic term more descriptively differentiates the Negro people from other dark-skinned strains of the human race. All these people originally inhabited South Africa, and is among the oldest sites of human habitation.

Over the thousands of years of humanity's existence, the environment has influenced how human beings have lived and developed. The conditions, circumstances, and influences surrounding human beings have affected how humanity has grown. There are two schools of thought in regards to the existence of humanity and the equality of the races.

Man: A Living and Existing Being

Basically over the thousands of years man; through the influence of the environment, which is the conditions, circumstances, and influence surrounding him and that affect his growth.

A human being, a primate; any of an order of mammals, including man, characterized especially by flexible hands and feet, each with five digits, which comprise an organism.

An organ or organism is any individual animal, having diverse organs and parts that function as a whole to maintain life and its activities. Man's organism comprises his limbs—an arm or leg or any projecting part—or forming an outgrowth or extension from a larger body to form together to make a whole.

Throughout history, from the beginning of time to today, man has adapted to the environment in which he lives.

The Theory of Evolution

The theory of evolution claims that the evolution of man was a process of development, as from a simple to a complex form or a gradual progressive change to the development of a species, an organism, from its original or primitive state to its present state. This involved many interrelated divisions that comprise man's life to date.

Organs and organism are parts of the human body and function by the structural adaptation of certain parts of the body to particular tasks.

Such functions constitute systems, such as muscular, skeletal, circulatory, respiratory, digestive, excretion, nervous, endocrine, reproductive, etc.

A study of organs, organisms, would deal with the study of anatomy and physiology. Physiology is the branch of biology dealing with the functions and vital processes of living organisms or their parts and system of organs.

Charles R. Darwin, 1809–1882, was born in Shrewsbury, England. He was educated at Cambridge and after studies was appointed by the crown as naturalist to the British ship *Beagle*, which made an expedition around the world. The voyage, which lasted five years, had a great influence on his future life.

He wrote a book titled *The Voyage of the Beagle*, which was a narrative of his cruise, which was published in 1840. After this voyage, Darwin was for several years occupied with the publication of the scientific results of the cruise.

One of his books was *The Origin of the Species*, but his most famous book was *The Descent of Man*, written in 1871, containing the speculation of the probable ancestors of man. The scientific world regarded this book as Darwin's chief contribution to a philosophical theory or a logical analysis of the principles that was fundamentally basic, but not clearly evident or expressed.

The theory, "natural selection," was formulated by Charles Darwin in 1859 to account for the origin of species, the human race. This "natural selection" theory was in suitable variations perpetuated by so-called "survival of the fittest," while others are eliminated in the famed struggle for existence. Both theories have had their spokesmen, many of whom were often more eloquent than scientific.

Darwin claims that all organisms face a constant struggle for existence. Individuals of a species must compete with each other, as well as with other species, for limited food supplies and shelter, also changes in eliminate and other physical factors.

No matter how well adapted the organism may be it can never become perfectly adapted to its environment because the environment is constantly changing. Darwin believed that continued structural modifications lead to the origin of species.

The theory of "natural selection" is widely accepted by most biologists as a plausible explanation of the mechanism of evolution.

Its chief fault, however, lies in the fact that it does not explain the origin of variations, the primary factor in evolution. Nor is it extensive enough to account for the evolution of all known traits of individual identity. These and many other difficulties have been encountered in the theory of "natural selection." Darwin's theories gave rise to one of the most controversial and debatable opposing opinions to a sharp disagreement in the scientific world.

The theory of evolution or organic evolution pertains to all forms of life, plant or animal, living or extinct, high or low, including man.

It claims that all forms of life have come from previously existing forms over long periods of earth's history, which they say is at the dawn of life on this planet probably some two thousand million years ago.

To support the theory of evolution, one fact is that all organisms descend from parental ones by various modes or reproduction. The general similarity between parents and offspring is hereditary. These hereditary factors can and do change, comparing living forms today with ones thousands of years ago.

Early man, for instance, differed greatly from the modern human race, and the same can be said of the early horses, etc. The animals and plants living today are thus regarded as interrelated, no matter how remote in the past their connection may prove to be. In most cases the origin of a new species required a very long time.

For example, the Neanderthal man is a designation of a form of primitive man of the Paleolithic period whose skeletal remains were first found in a valley in the Rhine province, Germany, in the year 1857.

Paleolithic man is of the types of man of an old world culture of the early Stone Age. During this period man developed flint, stone, and bone tools and lived by hunting, fishing, and gathering wild fruits.

Evolutionists claim that organic evolution is a slow process requiring hundreds of millions of years, but without its organic life would never have advanced beyond its first elementary creation.

The Mind

The mind is the seat of consciousness, thinking and perceiving. The mind determines a person's intellect and stores all of an individual's conscious experiences.

Knowledge is stored in the mind for use when needed and is a familiarity with a fact. In that all that has been perceived or grasped by the mind. The body of facts, principles, etc. accumulated by mankind.

Life is the time a person or thing is alive or exists. "Life, is Finite; meaning it has limits, to the point where something ends or must end."

Whereas, "Knowledge is Infinite; meaning it is lacking in limits or bounds, extending beyond measure or comprehension, without beginning or end."

One's environment is the condition surrounding a person. The culture of a given people in a given period of time has a bearing on the development of the mind. The will of an individual is the exercise of the power of making a reasoned choice or decision or of controlling one's own actions with a strong and fixed determination. A weak-willed person is lacking in moral strength and yields easily to temptation or the influences of others. People who are incapable of making rational decisions or adjusting to their environment might be said to have faulty thinking.

According to Aristotle and many other philosophers, the will is an appetitive, a desire to satisfy some craving of the body. The will tends inevitably toward good in general, but with regard to the choice of particular goods, it is said to be free.

Will and reason are both involved in freedom of choice, free will rising from the very fact of one's rationality, belief, or conviction. If adjustment in choice is stalemated or unresolved, the fact is registered in the consciousness. Thinking then will take care of this process more effectively than overt trial and error. The consciousness of having found a solution of adjustment and of effort to put this solution into effect is will. The act of thinking is to form in the mind one's opinion by consideration and arrive at a conclusion.

The phrase mind over matter has to do with the concept that matter is the opposite of the mind. Mind deals with intellect, whereas matter is whatever occupies space and is tangible.

The term mind is usually avoided by psychologists because they can find no distinctive organ or entity to identify. In that regard, facts of behavior are the only proper subject of study.

Our emotions, including both mental and physical reactions—love, hate, fear, anger, etc.—can affect our decision-making abilities. By giving in to any of these emotions is to sway one's capability of making the distinction between right and wrong.

Sodom was an ancient city near the Dead Sea that, according to biblical accounts, was destroyed by fire from heaven because of the wickedness of its inhabitants. It was destroyed for its wickedness, which included greed, a love for wealth and personal gain, and lust, a strong emotion that is conceived in the mind through the senses and results in sexual desire. Both greed and lust can sway a person's emotions and cause them to become corrupt.

Greed and lust are two specific emotions that can adversely affect a person. Greed is an avid desire for gain or wealth that causes one to want or take all that one can get with no thought of other people's needs. Greed is inconsistent with the moral law and will bring misery and distress upon every soul who does evil.

Acts 5:1-11 documents the story of Ananias and Sapphira, husband and wife, who were greedy and tried to trick God and the apostles. Both died at the feet of Peter because of their deceit.

Similarly, but different, lust is a strong emotion that is conceived in the mind, especially through the five senses. Lust is a desire to gratify the senses as in bodily appetite or sexual desire. This intense emotion can sway and divert one's concept of morals, even that of a strong-willed person.

A greedy person who desires nothing more than wealth will be sorely disappointed at the final judgment, for Jesus compared the difficulty of the wealthy reaching heaven with the impossibility of having a camel fit through the eye of a needle. In the New Testament we find the story of the rich young ruler who asked Jesus what he should do to be saved. Jesus told him to sell all that he had and give it to the poor that his treasure may be in heaven. Sadly, the rich young ruler was unwilling to give up his riches and position. The Bible also teaches that no man can serve two masters. One must choose between serving God or serving man and money.

Ultimately, the mind is the only portion of the body that can decide between right and wrong, good and evil. There are good and bad consequences associated with every decision. It is up to the conscious of the person to determine what decision he or she will make each day, each hour. One can choose to be moral or immoral, good or bad, righteous or wicked.

Socrates, 469–399 B.C.

A Greek philosopher, was born in Athens. He was primarily a philosopher, that is a person in the search for wisdom, a logical analysis of the principles underlying conduct, thought, knowledge, and the nature of the universe. Including a study of human morals, character, and behavior.

A man who wanted to know the meaning and purpose of men's lives and how human life should be rightly lived. Unlike other great Greek philosophers, like Plato, who was one of his pupils, he did not write books.

Socrates, turning from the external world to the study of what he called man's soul, which he defined as that in men by virtue of which he chooses to live rightly or wrongly, and that virtue of rightness of all kinds, is a sort of knowledge.

Socrates concludes that man naturally tends to go toward what is good. How then explain evil? Evil is do to error, that is to a mistakenly identifies good with his own personal comfort achieved at others expense. Thus, evil is not voluntary but involuntary, being due to a mistake in regard to what is good.

Be it known that many of these ancient Greek scholars like Plato 427–347 B.C. Philosopher; Xenophon 430–355 B.C. Historian; Aristotle 384–322 B.C. Philosopher, etc. lived during Roman Rule. Over time Rome gleaned much knowledge and information from these annexed nations.

The Five Senses

Sense is the ability of the nerves and the brain to receive and react to a stimulus that activates an organ or organism in the body. The five senses are sight, touch, taste, smell, and hearing, as distinct from the mind.

1. **Sight**—The sense of sight is produced through the eyes. The eye is connected with the brain by the optic nerve, which is located behind the nose. These organs are made up of systematically interrelated parts that, through perception, can mentally recognize an object as soon as it is seen.

2. **Touch**—This is the sense by which physical objects are felt. In earlier times, people would lay hands on a person to effect a cure. Nerve impulses to the brain are stimulated by the presence of outside physical forces and changes in the physical environment, including varying temperatures, which the brain registers as feelings of contact, pressure, cold, heat, and pain.
3. **Taste**—To discern or recognize flavors by putting a little in one's mouth. The sense of taste is stimulated by contact of a substance with the taste buds on the surface of the tongue and is capable of distinguishing between sweet, sour, salty, and bitter. The sensitivity to bitter is the greatest of all as would be expected from the protective nature of this sensation. Bitter things are usually rejected as soon as tasted.
4. **Smell**—Smell is to be or become aware of by means of the nose and the olfactory, which is a cranial nerve that arises in the mucous membrane within the upper part of the nose and transfers impulses concerned with the sense of smell to the forebrain, which detects scent or odor. Odor suggests a heavier emanation and, therefore, one that is more generally perceptible and more clearly recognizable. The specificity of odors is best illustrated by the ability of bloodhounds to recognize individuals by the volatile substances that cling to their bodies or articles of clothing. This personal odor suggests an individuality not duplicated in other persons.
5. **Hearing**—The external part of the ear is a projecting, skin-covered cartilage that has little or no function, although in some of the lower animals it is moveable and helps direct sound into the canal of the outer ear. Sounds are perceived through stimulation of auditory nerves in the ear out of which the brain forms meaningful noise, such as speech. Also, deep within the ear are structures that give us balance. The sense of equilibrium and balance in humans and other higher animals is dependent upon several interrelated mechanisms, such as eyesight and the intricate network of winding pathways in the inner ear. These senses affect the muscles, joints, and tendons of the body. On numerous occasions, observations of the wanderings of people and animals lost in snow and fog illustrate a tendency to move in a

circular path, because when vision is obscured no other mechanism compensates for the body's natural asymmetry, form of arrangement.

The complex structure of the human being from conception to maturity is comprehensible through continuing study of the body.

Chapter 11

Population of the Earth

God created and placed on earth three races, then separated them by placing them apart: Caucasoid, Mongoloid, and Negroid. God's purpose was in view of a future event to occur during a particular interval of time.

Each race in its own environment; all the conditions or being surrounded, and all the conditions, circumstances and influences surrounding and effecting the development of an organism or group of organisms. An organism is any form of animal or plant life. Anything with a very complex structure and parts which function not only in terms of one another but also in terms of the whole.

Life is that property of plants and animals that make it possible for them to take in food, get energy from it, grow, and adapt themselves to their surroundings and reproduce their kind. It is the quality that distinguishes a living animal or plant from inorganic matter or a dead organism.

A life cycle is the series of changes in form undergone by an organism in development from the earliest stage to the recurrence of the same stage in the next generation.

In human being's never ending quest for knowledge, a more detailed definition of life can be found under "biology" in the encyclopedia.

To sustain humans, their means of support, preservation, that which sustains life, nourishment, food. Sustentation depends on controlling the earth's population.

God created man to populate, enjoy, and care for His beautiful creation—Earth. In so doing God gave man the following command:

- Genesis 1:28—"And God blessed them, and God said unto them, Be fruitful, and multiply, and replenish the earth, and subdue it: and have dominion over the fish of the sea, and over the fowl of the air, and over every living thing that moveth upon the earth."

- Genesis 9:1—"And God blessed Noah and his sons, and said unto them, Be fruitful, and multiply, and replenish the earth."
- Genesis 22:17—"That in blessing I will bless thee, and in multiplying I will multiply thy seed as the stars of the heaven, and as the sand which is upon the sea shore; and thy seed shall possess the gate of his enemies."
- Genesis 28:3—"And God Almighty bless thee, and make thee fruitful, and multiply thee, that thou mayest be a multitude of people."
- Ezekiel 24:14—"I the Lord have spoken it: it shall come to pass, and I will do it; I will not go back, neither will I spare, neither will I repent; according to thy ways, and according to thy doings, shall they judge thee, saith the Lord God."
- Malachi 3:6—"For I am the Lord, I change not; therefore ye sons of Jacob are not consumed."

God, in His wisdom, did not place limitations on man, upon saying, "Be fruitful and multiply and replenish the Earth." Replenish means to make full or complete again, as by furnishing a new supply.

Saint Augustine (AD 354–430) was born at Tagaste, now Algeria. He preached that everything God made was good. Evil was a corruption of nature brought about by the exercise of the human will. That calamity and misfortune are necessary ingredients of human life.

This concept can be traced back to Marcus Aurelius, Emperor of Rome (AD 121–180) and Paul and others.

Since the creation of man, to this day, man, himself, morally, has not been able to deal with this problematic situation. Thus, the four horsemen of death, fire, famine, flood, and pestilence will come.

There is great loss of life in major natural disasters. The one that gives little or no warning of striking are floods and tidal waves.

China, the Netherlands, and India have been the scenes of the most devastating floods in recorded history. The modern Holland, because of its improved dikes, has been excluded from this group. Floods have caused great loss of life in India, with its density of population, as in China, the cause for the excessive number of deaths.

During the years 1348 to 1350, the Black Death, the plague occurred and covered Europe, killing 60 million persons. Plague in the Bible refers to any of various calamities sent down as divine punishment.

"One generation passeth away, and another generation cometh: but the earth abideth for ever" (Eccl. 1:4).

God created our world, but it is up to its people to care for it.

The Four Horsemen of the Apocalypse

The apocalypse is an imaginary name assumed by the writer of the various Jewish and Christian writings, especially the book of Revelations, about 200 BC–AD 300, depicting the ultimate destruction of evil and triumph of good. There are four riders on horses as follows:

1. **A rider on a white horse**—morally or spiritually pure, a conqueror with a crown and a bow; an archer clothed in white. A conqueror in this instance implies gaining control by war and moral force. Thus, bringing subject peoples under his rule.
2. **A rider on a red horse**—power was given to him that sat there on to take peace from the earth, and that they should kill one another, and there was given unto him a great sword. To take peace from the earth, the rider of the red horse will be the means to remove by armies annihilating each other, as peace is freedom from or stopping of war.
3. **A rider on a black horse**—this rider holds a pair of balances in his hand; scales for weight, fortune, fate, and justice. Seals, a shallow pan or pans of a balance to show how much a thing weights, with a known weight in one pan to determine the weight of the object in the opposing pan. The scales in this rider's hand could depict the weight of good and bad.
4. **A rider on a pale horse**—his name that sat on this horse was death, and hell followed after him. The power was given to them over the fourth part of the earth, which is hell and Hades. The power given to them was to kill evildoers with sword and with hunger, pestilence, and by wild beasts of the earth.

War was regarded by the Hebrews as essentially religious. Their God was the God of hosts, used biblically for a multitude of angels. In Bible scriptures, they overthrew Pharaoh and his hosts in the red sea. Also, there is a text that says, "Praise ye Him, and all His angels; praise ye Him, and all His hosts."

In Luke we read "And suddenly there was with the angel a multitude of the heavenly host praising God, and saying, Glory to God in the highest, and on earth peace, good will toward man."

"Horsemen of the Apocalypse"—Bas relief on Limoges Cathedral, France

The earliest evidence of warfare was by an archeological excavation dated back to the first primitive weapons found, presumably stones and clubs. Then on later digs, spears, throwing sticks, and bow and arrows, swords, and knives were found.

Afterwards, horses and chariots became a major part in ground warfare.

Recorded history begins with Greece and the Persian wars (504–466 BC). Sea warfare was originated during this time, but no recorded details exist.

War is a way of genocide, the systematic killing of people intended to destroy a nation. Even in today's world, nations are preparing defenses against a military attack or planning for a sudden, violent assault against a targeted nation.

There are four natural catastrophes that are effective in controlling the population of the earth: fire, flood, famine, and pestilence.

The apocalypse brings us God's certain promise that the long warfare between good and evil will end with the overthrow of Satan at the second coming of Christ to earth.

This prophecy is similar to other prophecies predicting future events, but it is also questionable in agreement with reality.

Armageddon

And he gathered them together into a place called; in the Hebrew tongue, Armageddon, (REV. 16:16).

Note, there is no documented, recorded proof of time and location of this Great Battle between Good and Evil, which is to be fought before the Day of Judgment (HEB. 9:27).

Armageddon is a fictitious name given to a gathering place, or Battle Ground, on which the final struggle between Good and Evil is to be fought, REV. 16:16.

The encyclopedia refers to Armageddon as the Battlefield of the "Apocalypse". The Apocalypse is any of various Jewish and Christian, pseudonymous writings, during the time; (c.200 B.C. and c. A.D. 300).

The Pseudonymous, (Pseudo) means having a fictitious name to be deceptively similar but not in actuality or reality.

It is noted that in current times battles are fought between nations, the Good Nation and the Evil Nation who are not designated by name, or race.

As the culture of mans mind, improves over time with the development; in this instance, Weapons of War. With nations vying for superiority in building these weapons it is noted that there are possibly five nations capable of getting involved in a war of this magnitude and survive.

The time and location of this Great War, will be implemented by man. As in past centuries a nation involved in violent, internal strife will go to war with a nation deemed unfriendly, or by an intriguing plot; or set-up, justifying a reason to declare war..

Thus as war takes precedence over internal strife, the nations media, newspapers, T.V., radio, etc., would be occupied with the war, thereby foregoing any previous pertinent civil events.

It is noted that the destructive power of weapons today are so powerful that a city, with its thousands of inhabitants can be totally demolished in a single attack.

The initial attack on a targeted city, or cities, would be devastating, leaving diplomacy out of the question.

The attacked nation immediate response; would be defense, then retaliation.

After the end of hostilities the people of the world, effected by this Great War suffering from the immense loss of life, property, and the utter devastation will be in shock, which will have a violent impact on the mind.

This may be the time of the Lord Jesus return to earth, in his Second Coming, when people on earth are praying for Salvation; the spiritual rescue from the consequences of sin.

Chapter 12

The Holy Spirit

Jesus to the Apostles
- Matthew 10:18-20—"And ye shall be brought before governors and kings for my sake, for a testimony against them and the Gentiles. But when they deliver you up, take no thought how or what ye shall speak: for it shall be given you in that same hour what ye shall speak. For it is not ye that speak, but the Spirit of your Father which speaketh in you."
- Luke 24:47, 49, 51—"And that repentance and remission of sins should be preached in his name among all nations, beginning at Jerusalem.… And, behold, I send the promise of my Father upon you: but tarry ye in the city of Jerusalem, until ye be endued with power from on high."
- John 3:13-15—"And no man hath ascended up to heaven, but he that came down from heaven, even the Son of man which is in heaven.… That whosoever believeth in him should not perish, but have eternal life." Just as Jesus was brought back to life and ascended to heaven, He left the promise with His followers that they, too, may share in His reward when He returns to this earth the second time.
- John 5:24, 28, 29—"Verily, verily, I say unto you, He that heareth my word, and believeth on him that sent me, hath everlasting life, and shall not come into condemnation; but is passed from death unto life.… all that are in the graves shall hear his voice, and shall come forth; they that have done good, unto the resurrection of life; and they that have done evil, unto the resurrection of damnation."
- John 8:51—"Verily, verily, I say unto you, If a man keep my saying, he shall never see death."
- John 14:26—"But the Comforter, which is the Holy Ghost, whom the

Father will send in my name, he shall teach you all things, and bring all things to your remembrance, whatsoever I have said unto you."
- Acts 1:9—"And when he had spoken these things, while they beheld, he was taken up; and a cloud received him out of their sight."
- Acts 2:1-6—"And when the day of Pentecost was fully come, they were all with one accord in one place. And suddenly there came a sound from heaven as of a rushing mighty wind, and it filled all the house where they were sitting. And there appeared unto them cloven tongues like as of fire, and it sat upon each of them. And they were all filled with the Holy Ghost, and began to speak with other tongues, as the Spirit gave them utterance. And there were dwelling at Jerusalem Jews, devout men, out of every nation under heaven. Now when this was noised abroad, the multitude came together, and were confounded, because that every man heard them speak in his own language."
- Acts 4:13—"Now when they saw the boldness of Peter and John, and perceived that they were unlearned and ignorant men, they marvelled; and they took knowledge of them, that they had been with Jesus."
- 1 Timothy 4:8—"Godliness is profitable unto all things, having promise of the life that now is, and of that which is to come."
- 1 Corinthians 15:20-23—"But now is Christ risen from the dead, and become the firstfruits of them that slept. For since by man came death, by man came also the resurrection of the dead. For as in Adam all die, even so in Christ shall all be made alive. But every man in his own order: Christ the firstfruits; afterward they that are Christ's at his coming."

The Early Christian Church

Some say that Paul created Christianity, but Jesus is the one who formed the early Christian church and is the Creator of the church. Paul wrote a large majority of the New Testament with all of the epistles or letters to the churches he had visited.

Jesus also called others to follow Him and to preach the gospel to the world. A few of the more prominent disciples are detailed here:
- **Barnabas**—He was a Levite and was born in Cyprus. His first recorded deed was the selling of his holdings and bringing the money to the

apostles after Pentecost, the seventh Sunday after Easter, celebrating the decent of the Holy Spirit upon the apostles. A little later he joined Paul on his first missionary journey.
- **John Mark**—He was the companion to Paul and Barnabas. Mark's mother lived in the home that became a meeting place for the apostles. Mark left Paul at Perga on the first mission trip. Mark joined Barnabas on a mission trip to Cyprus. He wrote the gospel of Mark around AD 70. It is recorded that Mark died the death of a martyr by being dragged through the streets of Alexandria.
- **Luke**—He was born in Antioch. He was a Gentile and physician in Greece, a man of great learning. Luke visited Paul during his many imprisonments. He remained with Paul about nine years. Nothing is known of Luke after Paul's death. He wrote the book of Luke around AD 90.
- **Timothy**—He was the son of a Greek father and a Jewish mother. He was converted to Christianity by Paul in the city of either Lystra or Derbe. Timothy was a chosen traveling companion and assistant to Paul. He worked among various churches of Asia, Macedonia, and Greece. When Paul felt death approaching, he summoned for Timothy.
- **Titus**—A Christian convert who became one of Paul's ablest assistants. He accompanied Paul to Jerusalem. Paul left him as administrator of church affairs in Crete. He was characterized by prudence, tact, and firmness.

Following are documented stories about the power of the apostles' work:
- Acts 9:36-41—Peter restores Dorcas to life.
- Acts 14:8-11—Paul heals a cripple at Lystra.
- Acts 19—Paul passed through Ephesus and found that certain disciples had not received the outpouring of the Holy Spirit, so he laid his hands on them and prayed, and the Holy Spirit came on them. They then spoke in tongues and prophesied.
- Acts 20:9-12—Paul restores Eutychus to life.
- Acts 28:7-9—Paul, after being shipwrecked, heals many disease on the island.

- 1 Corinthians 14:19—"Yet in the church I had rather speak five words with my understanding, that by my voice I might teach others also, than ten thousand words in an unknown tongue."

Many of the apostles suffered martyrdom, which is the death of a martyr. A martyr is someone who willingly suffers death rather than renounce his/her religion or beliefs, principle or cause; a person who is tortured or killed because of his or her beliefs.

Chapter 13

Summaries of This Book's Instances

Ark of the Covenant

An ornamental chest belonging to the children of Israel that was made of acacia wood and overlaid in gold. The chest measured two and a half cubits long by one and a half cubits in breath and depth. The contents of the chest consisted of the Ten Commandments, a pot of manna, and Aaron's rod that budded. The ark was constructed according to directions given to Moses (Exod. 25). After being captured once and moved around after that, the ark finally rested in the Most Holy Place of Solomon's temple in Jerusalem. What ultimately became of it is unknown. It has been assumed from uncertain evidence that it was destroyed with the temple by King Nebuchadnezzar of Babylon in 586 BC.

The ark contained the Ten Commandments written on two tables of stone. The first four are religious in nature; belief in one God, prohibition of idolatry, and keeping the Sabbath. The other six are moral laws governing behavior toward each other as human beings.

- Exodus 31:18—"And he gave unto Moses, when he had made an end of communing with him upon mount Sinai, two tables of testimony, tables of stone, written with the finger of God."
- Exodus 32:19—"And it came to pass, as soon as he came nigh unto the camp, that he saw the calf, and the dancing: and Moses' anger waxed hot, and he cast the tables out of his hands, and brake them beneath the mount."

- Exodus 34:1—"And the Lord said unto Moses, Hew thee two tables of stone like unto the first: and I will write upon these tables the words that were in the first tables, which thou brakest."

Solomon

Solomon was the king of Israel after the reign of his father, David. He was renowned for his wisdom and is known as the wisest person to ever live. He wrote the books of Proverbs, Ecclesiastes, and Song of Solomon. It is estimated that he wrote these books no earlier than the third century BC.

Queen of Sheba

The Queen of Sheba visited Solomon during his rule from *c.* 970–930 BC in Jerusalem to see if his fame was justified. She told him riddles, which the wise king solved. She was so amazed that she gave him gifts. Jesus referred to this visit to Solomon of the Queen of the South when reproving the scribes and Pharisees.

Sheba was the biblical name of an ancient country in southern Arabia, which is most likely the country of Ethiopia today. Ethiopia was a great power in the earliest period of recorded history. Its influence extended into Egypt. According to Ethiopian tradition, their sovereign, the Queen of Sheba, had a son, Menelik I, by King Solomon when she came to Jerusalem to meet Solomon. Years later it is said that Menelik visited his father in Jerusalem and brought back the ark of the covenant to Axum, the capital of the Axumite Kingdom. It is a sacred city to the Ethiopians.

Death and Hell

The body is the physical structure of human beings, as opposed to the soul, which is regarded as being the immortal or spiritual part of a person that enables a person to think and feel and makes that person unique.

The Hebrew word for hell is *sheol.* The Jews taught that the righteous and wicked dead lie in the grave after they pass away. To this realm are committed all souls at death, and there is no return. Some believe that the wicked immediately go to hell when they die; however, the Bible is clear as to the context of hell and death.

- Isaiah 38:10—"I said in the cutting off of my days, I shall go to the gates of the grave: I am deprived of the residue of my years."
- Psalm 49:14—"Like sheep they are laid in the grave; death shall feed on them; and the upright shall have dominion over them in the morning; and their beauty shall consume in the grave from their dwelling."
- Psalm 13:3—"Consider and hear me, O Lord my God: lighten mine eyes, lest I sleep the sleep of death."
- Job 7:8–10—"The eye of him that hath seen me shall see me no more: thine eyes are upon me, and I am not. As the cloud is consumed and vanisheth away: so he that goeth down to the grave shall come up no more. He shall return no more to his house, neither shall his place know him any more."
- Ecclesiastes 12:7—"Then shall the dust return to the earth as it was: and the spirit shall return unto God who gave it."
- Romans 5:12–14—"Wherefore, as by one man sin entered into the world, and death by sin; and so death passed upon all men, for that all have sinned: (For until the law sin was in the world: but sin is not imputed when there is no law. Nevertheless death reigned from Adam to Moses, even over them that had not sinned after the similitude of Adam's transgression, who is the figure of him that was to come."

There are countless stories of people who are taken to the hospital with no signs of life—no pulse, no heartbeat—who begin breathing again after medical intervention. Many of these individuals tell of their near-death experience. They describe seeing their body lying on the table. They describe seeing beautiful views and peaceful scenes of heaven. They describe angels and bright lights. The incident is fixed in their mind, and when they return to consciousness, they tell everyone of their experience.

Hallucination

Illusions, refer to mental deceptions which arise from various causes An illusion is a false mental image or conception which may be a misinterpretation of a real appearance or may be something imagined. It is also the apparent perception of sights, sounds, etc. that are not actually present.

Dream

A sequence of sensations, images, thoughts, etc., passing: through a sleeping mind. Something of an unreal beauty or charm.

As with hallucinations a dream will fade from memory in a short period of time. A dream to be remembered, must be recorded soon after the mental vision or trance, which is of a altered consciousness.

So how does one explain a near-death experience? It is difficult to understand how the mind works, but regardless of what type of dream or hallucination they may have had, people who go through near-death experiences do not leave their body and go to heaven or hell.

Forgiveness

Jesus work on earth, given to Him by the Father, involved forgiving people of their sins and calling them to sin no more. Through His perfect life, Jesus made it possible to forgive everyone's sins so that all may receive the gift of eternal life and the pardon of sins. The forgiveness of sins is available to everyone, but one must ask to be forgiven. When one's sins are forgiven, one is pardoned from the penalty of sin—death.

The following texts talk about forgiveness:
- Genesis 50:17—Pray for forgiveness.
- Psalm 86:5—Call upon the Lord for forgiveness.
- Jeremiah 31:34—Repent and the Lord will forgive you.
- Matthew 6:12—In the Lord's prayer, Jesus says, "And forgive us our debts, as we forgive our debtors."
- Matthew 18:21, 22—When someone asks for forgiveness, one must forgive that person.
- Luke 6:37—"Judge not, and ye shall not be judged: condemn not, and ye shall not be condemned: forgive, and ye shall be forgiven."
- Luke 17:3—"Take heed to yourselves: If thy brother trespass against thee, rebuke him; and if he repent, forgive him."
- 1 John 1:9—"If we confess our sins, he is faithful and just to forgive us our sins, and to cleanse us from all unrighteousness."

Heaven

The name paradise is often used to denote heaven. In the Old Testament heaven mainly refers to the material world about the earth. Heaven is explained by the fact that the Jews divided heaven into three parts of which the first was the air or atmosphere, the second the firmament, the sky in which the sun, moon, and stars are fixed, and the third was the abode of God and His angels.

Jesus compared the difficulty of the wealthy reaching heaven to that of sending a camel through the eye of a needle. When the rich young ruler came to see Jesus, and Jesus urged him to follow Him, the sorrowful young ruler was unwilling to give up his riches and he turned and walked slowly away. The Bible teaches that no one can serve two masters, meaning no one can serve God and their own desires. Everyone, rich and poor alike, will be judged to determine who is fit for heaven and who is not.

Religion is a belief in a divine or superhuman power or powers to be obeyed and worshiped as the creator and ruler of the universe. An expression of such a belief in conduct and ritual.

To be a morally good and worthy person in God's eyes, to be accepted into God's kingdom, and to receive His grace and mercy at the final judgment, humans do not have to be devoted to Judaism, Christianity, Islamism, Buddhism, or Hinduism. To be worthy of God's love be just in your conduct, believe in one true God.

In the Hebrew religion, in early times, tithes were first fruits of the season. Later the tithe, in kind of its value in money, was taken. Then in times of decadence the payment of tithes was neglected. The Hebrew Pharisees accepted garden herbs. It was taught that withholding tithes was equivalent to robbing God.

Tithe was distributed to charities, worthy causes, and religious necessities.

In Christianity, Jesus and His apostles preached, collected tithes, when appropriate, sustained themselves, built churches, gathered converts, and promulgated the Christian religion.

To have and retain faith in one's God take a lesson from the Son of God, Jesus Christ. Every day He prayed to the Father, thanking Him for His guidance and bringing Him through the day.

Every day in your life thank God for any event, happening, occurrence, or predicament that turned out well. Also, thank God for every incident that did not turn out to your satisfaction, advantage, justification, etc., for this failure is a lesson.

Thank God for these stumbling blocks. A lesson learned by hard knocks are not easily forgotten. Cursing a bad happening delights the devil.

Faith

Faith is a basic element in the religious awareness of one's own feelings, and one which fills a dominant place in Christian life.

Faith comes to signify a personal, deep conviction, associated with humble self-surrender to the divine. Faith must be regarded as the agreement to the official teaching of the church.

Faith healing, the real or alleged cure of disease by a supernatural power through the Faith of the sufferer or of others on his behalf. This may be considered as the only curable force or as a supplement to natural means.

This belief is as old as magic and older than medicine. It came into Christianity with the records of the healing miracles of Jesus. In the Apostolic Age, the ability to use this healing force was regarded as a "Gift of the Spirit", (1 COR. 12 :9).

Faith – Hope – Charity

Faith is the unquestioning belief that does not require proof. A belief in God or a system of religious beliefs, with complete trust, confidence and reliance.

Hope is a confident expectation of something that will happen, and of something desired. A feeling that what is wanted will happen. A thing on which one may base some hope.

Charity, in Christian Theology is the love of God for man or of man for his fellow man. A voluntary giving of money or other help to those in need. An act of Good Will or affection.

Angel

An angel is one of a class of spiritual beings, attendants of God, an attendant or guardian spirit. A race of spiritual beings of a nature exalted above that of humanity. It is their office to serve God and worship Him. They are agents of God's providence of humanity, as well as the instrument of His punishment.

The term archangel is given an angel belonging to the higher order of heavenly bodies from its Greek meaning chief angel. In the Old Testament the conception of supernatural beings, derived from the beliefs and customs of the Greeks and Persians while the Hebrews were in exile in Babylon. Archangels are the highest place in the ranks of angels by the New Testament.

Two archangels, Michael and Gabriel, are specifically named in the Bible. Others, Jeremiel, Phaltiel, Raphael, and Uriel. Satan, as a proper name and as prince of fallen angels, is first mentioned in Job 1:6–12.

Two New Testament teachings regarding angels are not as in the Old Testament, mediators between God and men, that is reserved for Christ or the Holy Spirit.

The archangel Michael is the Warrior of Light. The greatest Angel in all Christian, Jewish, and Islamic writings. Whose name means who is as God, with the sword of righteousness.

Michael is the special guardian of the Hebrews. He disputed with Satan over the body of Moses and fought with the dragon in heaven. As the leader and head of the good angels, He defeated Lucifer and the army of evil angels who disobeyed the Supreme Being.

Gabriel is one of the seven archangels who are of the highest rank in the hierarchy of angels. In the Old Testament his name is only mentioned in Daniel 8:15 and 9:21. In the New Testament he appears before Mary (Luke 1:26). He also appears as a messenger to Zacharias (Luke 1:8–20).

Since Gabriel appears as the revealing angel, it is possible that it was this biblical representation that formed the basis of the Mohammedan conception of the archangel as the messenger who delivered the Koran from Allah to the prophet Mohammed.

Trinity

The Greek concept of the Logos, or Word of God, dates back to 475 BC and entered into the Christian theology and to the way of combining unity of being with multiplicity of persons. This Greek philosophy produced the Trinity, which affirmed the existence of three persons within the substance of one undivided godhead.

This early Greek philosophy of the Trinity, three gods in one, was the concept, accepted at the time, by the Roman Catholic Church, in that Jesus Christ is God as well as man and also the Spirit is God. A conference of bishops was held to perfect a doctrine for the church. The doctrine was that of the Trinity, which was made official by the Council of Nicaea in AD 325 and was given a definitive statement by the Council of Constantinople in AD 382.

The Bible reveals the godhead as comprised of three distinct, not alike, individuals. God is God. He is the head of the seat of logic, the science of correct reasoning that describes relationships of something that is not definitely known, understood, or identified.

Monotheistic religions and idealistic philosophies recognize God as a Supreme Being, the Creator and Sustainer of the universe. The Bible teaches us that the God of heaven is the only person humanity owes worship to. There is no other god; He is the first and last. The dictionary defines god as "any of various beings conceived of as supernatural, immortal, and having special powers over the lives and affairs of people and the course of nature." A deity, a god or goddess.

Jesus is the second person of the Trinity. It was recognized in early Christian theology that Jesus was the incarnation of the Logos, the Word of God, and by so doing kept Christianity a monotheistic religion that also provided justification for worship of Christ as the active expression of divine thought and will.

- Matthew 3:17—"And lo a voice from heaven, saying, This is my beloved Son, in whom I am well pleased."
- Matthew 16:16—"And Simon Peter answered and said, Thou art the Christ, the Son of the living God."
- Luke 22:41, 42—"And he was withdrawn from them about a stone's cast, and kneeled down, and prayed, saying, Father, if thou be willing, remove this cup from me: nevertheless not my will, but thine, be done."
- John 1:1-3—"In the beginning was the Word, and the Word was with God, and the Word was God. The same was in the beginning with God. All things were made by him; and without him was not any thing made that was made."
- John 13:13—"Ye call me Master and Lord: and ye say well; for so I am."
- 1 Timothy 2:5—"For there is one God, and one mediator between God and men, the man Christ Jesus."

In the New Testament the doctrine of the Holy Spirit was developed and the basis for the concept of the Trinity was laid down. The Holy Spirit, otherwise referred to as the Holy Ghost, is the third person in the Trinity. The question as to whether the Spirit proceeds from the Father alone or the Father and Son contributed toward the separation of the Roman and Eastern churches.

The work of the Holy Spirit is to sanctify or make holy the people of God and to comfort God's followers and lead them into truth. His personality is implied in the baptismal formula. If the Father and Son are distinct person, so must be the Holy Spirit. All three persons were present at the baptism of Jesus.

- Luke 24:49—"And, behold, I send the promise of my Father upon you: but tarry ye in the city of Jerusalem, until ye be endued with power from on high."
- John 15:26—"But when the Comforter is come, whom I will send unto you from the Father, even the Spirit of truth, which proceedeth from the Father, he shall testify of me."
- Genesis 1:28—"And God blessed them, and God said unto them, be fruitful, and multiply, and replenish the earth, and subdue it: and have dominion over the fish of the sea, and over the fowl of the air, and over every living thing that moveth upon the earth."
- Genesis 9:1—"And God blessed Noah and his sons, and said unto them, Be fruitful, and multiply, and replenish the earth."
- Genesis 22:17—"That in blessing I will bless thee, and in multiplying I will multiply thy seed as the stars of the heaven, and as the sand which is upon the sea shore; and thy seed shall possess the gate of his enemies."
- Genesis 28:3—"And God Almighty bless thee, and make thee fruitful, and multiply thee, that thou mayest be a multitude of people."

Not only do people question where human beings came from but the very existence of the universe is drawn into the creation versus evolution debate. As we study the universe and the totality of all the things that exist in it, there are three theories to consider: 1) it has always existed; 2) the universe created itself; 3) it was created.

The first theory has been rejected by the scientific community. The second theory is impossible based on philosophy. If the universe hasn't always existed, how could it have been around to do the creating? The scientific, theological, and reasonable conclusion leads one to believe in the third theory, that the universe was created.

Laws of Moses

Early Christians used the term the "law" for the whole Old Testament. This is a result of their upbringing and the instruction from the priests, prophets, and Pharisees. Before the law of Moses was instituted, there was a form of retaliation to deal with crime and punishment. The law of Moses, which is contained in the first five books of the Bible, but especially in the book of Leviticus, was instituted to bring order to the Israelites, but over time it became a burden of rituals in the form of cooking, cleaning, and worshipping because of the regulations of the Pharisees. When people sinned, they were to bring a sin offering to the priest for atonement for their sins. The offering was cattle, sheep, or grain.

Offerings and Sacrifice

Sacrifice is the act of offering the life of a person or animal, in order to regain the good will or appease a God or Deity.

The first seven chapters of the Prophet Leviticus, sets forth most explicitly the laws for Sacrificial Offerings.

These laws were set by God in his Covenant with Moses on Mount Sinai (Exodus 19:1–24). An early example of an offering is Noah's first act, after leaving the ark, was to build an alter to God, and offer Burnt Offerings of every clean beast and fowl.

These offerings were not of the nature of expiation, as to make amends for wrong doing, but rather in recognition of a bond between God and the person who tendered the offering.

Another example of an expiatory offering were to Job 42:8. This offering to Job was by his three friends, Eliphaz, Bildad, and Shuhite, was for their wrong, thoughtless, treatment of him during his prolonged suffering.

The Burnt-Offering, the meat or meal offering, at meal times is seeking divine favor and giving thanks to God for the food.

The Peace Offering is a sign of Communion with God. The Sin Offering and Trespass Offering in expiation of Sin. These Levitical Offerings were later referred to as imperfect sacrifices.

A Ceremonial Offering is a formal function established by custom, which is the usual practice or habitual way of behaving, carried on by tradition. A Ceremonial Offering could be by authority; the power or right of a person to give commands.

Ceremonial occasions are usually a solemn ceremony, as a wedding, or a religious rite.

God's Plan to Obtain a New Covenant With Humanity

If the first covenant had been faultless then there would be no occasion for a second (Jer. 31:31–34; Heb. 8:7; Heb 10:9, 10).

God designed a detailed plan, in a realistic way, of bringing the people of earth into the spiritual realm of His kingdom. And to redeem (to set free) by paying a ransom, a price, to redeem the curse of the grave and everlasting death.

Deuteronomy 11:26–28—"Behold, I set before you this day a blessing and a curse;

- Bless, is to make or declare Holy by a spoken fixed formula of words ie. "God Bless You", or a sign; as "The Sign of the Cross," a gesture, over or upon a person or thing. To signify, as meaning to keep and protect from harm.
- Blessed is enjoying great happiness and bringing comfort and joy, also Blessed are those dead whose souls are in Heaven
- Blessing is the Prayer of one who Blesses. A gift of divine favor as an unexpected occurrence that brought happiness or contentment at an appropriate time.
- Grace, a short prayer in which a Blessing is asked, or thanks are given, before or after a meal.
- A blessing, if ye obey the commandments of the Lord your God, which I command you this day: And a curse, if ye will not obey the commandments of the Lord your God, but turn aside out of the way which I command you this day, to go after other gods, which ye have not known."
- Romans 5:12—"Wherefore, as by one man sin entered into the world, and death by sin; and so death passed upon all men, for that all have sinned."

- Ezekiel 24:14—"I the Lord have spoken it: it shall come to pass, and I will do it; I will not go back, neither will I spare, neither will I repent; according to thy ways, and according to thy doings, shall they judge thee, saith the Lord God."
- The old covenant required an offering of sacrifice in God's command to Abraham (Gen. 15:9) and to David (Ps. 50:5).
- Jeremiah 31:31, 32—"Behold, the days come, saith the Lord, that I will make a new covenant with the house of Israel, and with the house of Judah: Not according to the covenant that I made with their fathers."

A sacrifice of expiation, the offering of life of animal, plant, or human or some material possession, etc. to a deity (the state of being a god), as in appeasement or reverence.

To bring redemption of God's curse and to make a new covenant can only be obtained through God's own righteous law as every word from the mouth of God is final and not retractable.

In accordance to God's law, as taught by Moses and the prophets, an atonement for sin or wrongdoing required a sacrifice to reconcile God to man. God's righteous law and man's conceptualism of God's law required a new covenant (Heb. 8:6-13). The new covenant foretold by Jeremiah.

The sin offering, sacrifice, neither by the blood of goats and calves by the Levites, the tribe descended from Levi and afterwards the Israelite priestly class, offerings were the imperfect sacrifice (see Lev. 1-4 and Heb. 9:12).

The ultimate perfect sacrifice is possible only through the perfect Savior, Jesus Christ. The Lamb of God, offered in sacrifice once only and for all, rather than daily as by the Aaronic, pertaining to Aaron, the son of Amram and brother of Moses.

Fortunately, Jesus came to this earth and redeemed His people so that the rituals and laws of Moses were no longer necessary for the forgiveness of sins. The following quote was taken from the concordance in the King James Version Bible under the heading "Resurrection": "Jesus died on the cross for the redemption of a race of sinners condemned by the laws given to Moses by God. Redemption, denotes release or freedom upon payment of a price, not only of the soul, but embraces as well redemption of the body."

God's plan to obtain a new covenant with man would go beyond and surpass even the pagan's cruel sacrifices. This by sacrificing a Lord, a deity, His only Son, to die on a cross, to be crucified.

Hebrews 9:16-18—"For where a testament is, there must also of necessity be the death of the testator. For a testament is of force after men are dead: otherwise it is of no strength at all while the testator liveth. Whereupon neither the first testament was dedicated without blood." (See also Heb. 9:19, 20).

The plan and purpose was to bring about a new covenant and not according to the Old Testament. This would require a plan with a specific end in view and with good results or effects.

This to be accomplished by giving the people on earth a Lord, a deity, but of a corporeal body, of a material, not spiritual nature, that could be understood. Also, a way, through teachings, to bring all people of all nations into His kingdom.

The cause was that Jesus, the Son of God, would be sent as an agent of God to be born of man to bring about a righteous new covenant.

In order to obtain a new covenant with man and bring people of earth into the spiritual realm of His kingdom, the details of the plan may have been formulated centuries before being implemented. As Jesus' time on earth coincided with the domination and building of the Roman Empire.

Prayer

Praying is a spiritual communication with God. It is an opportunity to present solemn requests before God in a humble and sincere manner. God allows all things to happen, both good and bad, for a purpose. Therefore, humans must yield to God's will. The burden of misfortune should not be prescribed to God; it is because of the sinful world we live in and the work of Satan that misfortune comes upon people.

Prayer involves talking to God, in hopes that a specific result will be brought about. Some religions use rote prayers as a means of communicating with God. The Catholic Church promotes the use of rosary beads, a string of beads that are used to keep count of the number of prayers said and in what order. There is typically one large bead and ten small beads, which stands for ten Hail Marys, one Our Father, and one "glory be to the Father." Other religious groups use a string of beads in a similar way. For Tibetan Buddhists, like the rosary, they count their prayers. But they use a prayer wheel, which is a revolving drum with prayers written on it.

Prophecy of the Messiah

The book of Deuteronomy contains the prophecy of the coming of the Messiah. "The Lord thy God will raise up unto thee a Prophet from the midst of thee, of thy brethren, like unto me; unto him ye shall hearken" (Deut. 18:15). Deuteronomy 6:4–9 is recited every day by Jews all over the world. It was these verses that Jesus quoted when the Pharisees demanded to know the greatest commandment in the law. And Jesus said unto them "thou shalt love the Lord thy God with all thine heart, and with all thy soul, and with all thy might" (Deut. 6:5).

Resurrection, Eternal Life

While Jesus was on this earth, He instructed His disciples to tell others of the love of God the Father in heaven. Jesus prayed for His disciples and taught them so that they could teach others. After His resurrection, He called His disciples to take the good news of salvation to the whole world.

Eternal Life (Bible) Perpetual, Everlasting

- Matthew 25:46 And these shall go away into everlasting punishment; but the righteous into Life Eternal.
- Mark 3:29 But he that shall blaspheme against the Holy Ghost hath never forgiveness, but is in danger of eternal damnation.
- John 3:15 That whosoever believeth in Him should not perish but have eternal life.
- John 10:28 And I give unto them eternal life, and they shall never perish, neither shall any man pluck them out of my hand.

2 Corinthians 4:18 While we look not at the things which are seen, but at the things which are not seen; for the things which are seen are temporal; but the things which are not seen are eternal

Soul (Dictionary) Websters New World

An entity; a thing that has definite individual existence.

An entity which is regarded as being the immortal or spiritual part of the person and, though having no physical or material reality, is credited with the functions of thinking and willing, and hence determining all behavior.

Soul (The American College Encyclopedic Dictionary)

The principle of life, feeling, thought, and action in man, regarded as a distinct entity separate from the body, and commonly held to be separate in existence from the body.

The spiritual part of man as distinct from the physical. The spiritual part of man regarded in its moral, or as believed to survive death and be subject to happiness or misery in a life to come.

Soul (Bible) Concordance, verbatim

The living soul of Genesis 2:7 is a physical body into which the breath of life has been divinely breathed.

Two views prevail concerning the relationship of the soul to the body, one which holds man to consist of body and soul (Matthew 10:28) and a second which takes the position that man may be considered as consisting of body, soul and spirit (1 Thessalonians 5:23).

The soul is sometimes called the inner man (Romans 7:22; 2 Corinthians 4:16; Ephesians 3:16) and inward parts (Psalm 5:9).

Sin

The Bible declares that sin had its origin in our universe with the fall of Satan. "And the great dragon was cast out, that old serpent, called the Devil, and Satan, which deceiveth the whole world: he was cast out into the earth, and his angels were cast out with him" (Rev. 12:9).

From the beginning Satan was allowed to make a choice, and he chose to seek authority for himself and disregard God's laws. After he and the other angels were thrown out of heaven, he began carrying out his evil purposes and plans in regards to tricking the human race.

"And the Lord God commanded man, saying, Of every tree of the garden thou mayest freely eat: But of the tree of the knowledge of good and evil, thou shalt not eat of it: for in the day that thou eatest thereof thou shalt surely die"

(Gen. 2:16, 17). Sin entered the human race because of the disobedience of Adam and Eve (Rom. 5:12–21).

After Adam and Eve ate the fruit, God said to Adam, "Because thou hast hearkened unto the voice of they wife, and hast eaten of the tree, of which I commanded thee, saying, Thou shalt not eat of it: cursed is the ground for thy sake; in sorrow shalt thou eat of it all the days of thy life" (Gen. 3:17). To this day, gardens are plagued with locust, drought, flood, fire, and pestilence. The result of this initial sin was death.

"Wherefore, as by one man sin entered into the world, and death by sin; and so death passed upon all men, for that all have sinned: (For until the law sin was in the world: but sin is not imputed when there is no law. Nevertheless death reigned from Adam to Moses, even over them that had not sinned after the similitude of Adam's transgression, who is the figure of him that was to come" (Rom. 5:12–14). This text clearly states that the penalty of sin is death.

Christ's sacrifice on the cross gave us a way to overcome sin through grace: "For sin shall not have dominion over you: for ye are not under the law, but under grace" (Rom. 6:14).

The seven deadly sins, according to Christian tradition, are as follows:
- **Pride**—an overly high opinion of oneself; exaggerated self-esteem
- **Covetousness**—want of something that another person has
- **Lust**—a desire to gratify the senses, sexual desire, an overmastering desire
- **Anger**—is broadly applicable to feelings of resentment or revenge from the cause of an injury or mistreatment and showing a desire to fight back, thereby self-control is lost
- **Gluttony**—a person who greedily eats too much or a person with a great capacity for something
- **Envy**—a feeling of ill will, jealousy, discontent of another's possessions or advantage that one desires
- **Slothfulness**—a slow and lazy person with a dislike to work or exert oneself

Satan, the Devil and Temptation

From the beginning, Satan is spoken of as a person, a personification of evil forces. Primitive and oriental cultures recognized the existence of vast numbers of spirits, good and bad and neutral. The concept of angels and demons passed over to Judaism and Christianity. The devil is the chief evil spirit, a supernatural being subordinate to and the foe of God, and the tempter of humanity. Satan is the world prince of all devils.

When Jesus was tempted three times by the devil, He answered by quoting Scripture. He turned to God for His defense against the devil. When human beings are tempted to do wrong, they should call on the Lord to drive the devil away, and Satan will flee, for he cannot stand the word of God.

Demonology is the study of demons and evil spirits. Nature-based religions often made provisions for placating harmful spirits by offering them worship and sacrifice. The people of Babylon and Assyria believed there was a consistent battle between the spirits of light and the demons of darkness. The Egyptians and the Greeks believed that good and evil spirits were in constant battle for power. In early times sacrifice of youths and maidens was practiced to placate these evil gods. Demonology also figures in Judaism, Christianity, and Mohammedanism. In these religions demons are viewed as creatures that are subject to the will of God.

The devil is a supernatural being who is the enemy of God. Also known as Satan, Beelzebub, the prince of the devils, Lucifer, and the chief of the fallen angels. The devil is the tempter of humanity. A very wicked or malevolent person; a person who is mischievous, energetic, reckless, cruel, diabolical and wild.

Temptation is a fact or state of being tempted, especially to do evil. To entice or allure to do something unwise or wicked; to seduce is literally to lead astray. To tempt is to attract by holding out the probability of gratification or advantage, often in the direction of that which is wrong or imprudent. Satan is the greatest tempter. He seeks to lure people into degeneration by corruption of their moral character. William Shakespeare wrote; "The devil can cite Scripture for his purpose."

Judgment

Everyone who has ever lived on the face of the earth will be judged by God and deemed righteous or unrighteous. Everyone has a choice to make as to whether they will follow God or Satan, and they will be judged according to this decision. At the final judgment both wicked and righteous will agree with

God's verdict. No begging, entreaty, supplication, or prayer at the final judgment will change God's verdict.

It is manifest in several passages of the New Testament that the destinies of humans are fixed by their actions during life and that death closes their account.

The apostles were aware of this teaching, and they helped to spread the word after Christ's death. They knew that it was their commission to warn others of the coming judgment, as everyone is to be judged based on the "light" and knowledge that one has when Christ returns. It is said that what one sow's on earth, he will reap at the final judgment.

Matthew 12:36, 37—"But I say unto you, That every idle word that men shall speak, they shall give account thereof in the day of judgment. For by thy words thou shalt be justified, and by thy words thou shalt be condemned."

- Matthew 16:26, 27—"For what is a man profited, if he shall gain the whole world, and lose his own soul? or what shall a man give in exchange for his soul?"
- Matthew 25:41—"Then shall he say also unto them on the left hand, Depart from me, ye cursed, into everlasting fire, prepared for the devil and his angels."
- John 5:22—"For the Father judgeth no man, but hath committed all judgment unto the Son."
- John 14:6—"Jesus saith unto him, I am the way, the truth, and the life: no man cometh unto the Father, but by me."
- Romans 3:10—"As it is written, There is none righteous, no, not one."
- Galatians 6:5—"For every man shall bear his own burden." In the Old Testament, a burden was an oracle of divine utterance. In the New Testament, a burden signifies the woes and tribulations of life. The severity of the burden or hardship can be oppressive, wearisome, annoying, or tedious to the mind and/or body. As moral humans we cannot see the scope of a specific burden.
- Galatians 6:7—"Be not deceived; God is not mocked: for whatsoever a man soweth, that shall he also reap."
- Hebrews 9:27—"And as it is appointed unto men once to die, but after this the judgment."

- 2 Peter 2:4—"For if God spared not the angels that sinned, but cast them down to hell, and delivered them into chains of darkness, to be reserved unto judgment."
- Revelation 20:10, 12–15—"And the devil that deceived them was cast into the lake of fire and brimstone, where the beast and the false prophet are, and shall be tormented day and night for ever and ever.... And I saw the dead, small and great, stand before God; and the books were opened: and another book was opened, which is the book of life: and the dead were judged out of those things which were written in the books, according to their works. And the sea gave up the dead which were in it; and death and hell delivered up the dead which were in them: and they were judged every man according to their works. And death and hell were cast into the lake of fire. This is the second death. And whosoever was not found written in the book of life was cast into the lake of fire."

The final judgment is final. It is unchangeable. God calls everyone to decision who they will follow—God or Satan. The Bible is given to all people to edify us and prepare us for the final judgment when the wheat will be separated from the chaff, representing the separation of the righteous from the wicked. Satan cannot destroy a person whom God has created. Only God can destroy His creation and cleanse the earth of all wickedness.

Conclusion

In the writing of this book and by study and research, the author has gained knowledge and wisdom. It is hoped that you, as a reader, have benefited as well.

We invite you to view the complete
selection of titles we publish at:

www.ASPECTBooks.com

Scan with your mobile
device to go directly
to our website.

Please write or email us your praises, reactions,
or thoughts about this or any other book we publish at:

P.O. Box 954
Ringgold, GA 30736

info@ASPECTBookscom

ASPECT Books titles may be purchased in bulk for
educational, business, fund-raising, or sales promotional use.
For information, please e-mail:

BulkSales@ASPECTBooks.com

Finally, if you are interested in seeing
your own book in print, please contact us at

publishing@ASPECTBooks.com

We would be happy to review your manuscript for free.

www.ingramcontent.com/pod-product-compliance
Lightning Source LLC
Chambersburg PA
CBHW070542170426
43200CB00011B/2512